You Are A Leaf On The Soul Tree

Spiritual Alchemy &
The Tree of Life

Segolene King

To order more copies or to contact the author,
visit: www.vividpublishing.com.au/theinsightseries

Copyright © 2025 Segolene King
ISBN: 978-1-923078-58-1

Published by Vivid Publishing
A division of Fontaine Publishing Group
P.O. Box 948, Fremantle
Western Australia 6959
www.vividpublishing.com.au

A catalogue record for this
book is available from the
National Library of Australia

With eternal gratitude to the many fingers of the invisible hand which guided my journey, and the leaves who shared their Soul Tree Wisdom along the way.

To T.C. for giving me a home and amazing opportunities
To L.S. for ongoing friendship and reality checks
To L. M. for generous support and kindness,
To F. R. for the joy and skilful orchestrating.
To T.K. for making my heart burst
To Amy for the gift of radiance and ease
To Michael, my love, my champion, and opener of doors.

CONTENTS

~~~

CHAPTER 1

The Call

~ ~ ~

I perched precariously on the ledge of my 6th-floor window. It was the first snow of winter and my breath formed clouds that disappeared into the night sky. I was fifteen, and almost ready to give up on life, almost... I watched the snowflakes floating in slow motion amidst the dim city lights, blanketing the moment in sacred silence... And I thought, "This is a beautiful night to die".

I didn't jump (obviously). And though tragic it may seem, let me tell you: That night was when my life truly began. It was a crossroads, a moment of choice. At the low point of wanting to abandon life, I could have chosen anything: give up, give in, ignore, pretend or jump. I refused any of these options. An invisible hand, a tangible force, seemed to hold me back as I considered the snowy abyss below me. After minutes on the edge, I decided to live, for real this time. If I was going to stick with life, then I was going to make it worthwhile. I didn't know where I was heading, but I knew a course change was necessary. I grabbed my life in my own hands for the very first time. Some people never come to face this sort of life crisis. Others do, but choose the easy road towards the sleep of the spiritually amnesic Soul. I chose to wake up.

Why did I end up on that snowy window ledge? Was my existence so terrible that I could no longer bear it? No. My life was, according to all appearances, perfectly normal. Not ideal, not amazing, but not a nightmare either. There were issues, of course, but whose life doesn't? Yet it appeared all so… lifeless. The prospect of continuing on a path towards the normal adult life that everyone and everything expected filled me with emptiness. I could not explain it, but I also could not deny it. If this was good enough for everyone else, why not for me?

One question kept quietly pulsing within me "Is there more to life than this?" I looked around my little world for an answer, a clue pointing to that mysterious "something more"… but found nothing reflected there to show me the way. Everyone's life around me continued as normal. Society offered a range of *normal* expected pathways into adulthood, to *normal* jobs, *normal* ambitions and *normal* feelings. All the while, I wondered: what is the purpose of it all? Why do we do what we do? Perhaps what I was feeling was not *normal!* Was there something wrong with me? I remember meeting a girl about my age at a party on Saturday night. I spent a good hour pouring out my existential questioning to her: What is the purpose of living? Why are we here? What are all these people doing with their lives? Where are we all going? *WHAT IS THE POINT OF IT ALL??* I am afraid to say I scared her away with my big, edge-of-the-cliff questions. Sometimes I wasn't sure if there was something wrong with me, or something wrong with everyone else. Regardless, I didn't seem to fit with the normal future projected ahead of me, and it filled me with misery. The question - pulsing, pulsing -did not go away.

Later in life, I would learn that these questions, which appear from within and refuse to go away, are in fact answers waiting to be received and made manifest in our consciousness. The question is the medium that creates a space within us to receive the answer we need, even when we didn't know we needed it. This question "Is there something more to life than this?" was, in truth, the answer knocking at my door: "Yes, there is more to life". It was a calling. But…where was that call coming from?

We all get called to something in our lives. Everyone has a place and a path that they will naturally feel drawn to, if they listen to their heart's truth. Some people are born to be bakers, some people are born to be artists, some people are born to be mothers or fathers, some people are born to live off-grid in the forest. Some people are born to be accountants, some to be soldiers and some people are born to be misfits and edge-dwellers. Some are called to do great things while others are called to live quiet lives. Everyone belongs with a particular life path that will be true to them, but not everyone hears the call to something spiritual, beyond the realm of our material, third-dimensional existence. Some people feel a sense of calling early in life and a rare minority may even be born with it innately assertive within them. Others experience their call after 'trying on' the mundane materialistic existence promoted by our consumer societies, eventually finding themselves utterly unfulfilled and empty. For those people, regardless of how postcard-perfect their material success may be, or how many social expectation boxes they ticked, they still feel a sense of something missing. Others experience the call in middle-age, when careers have been taken to their natural conclusion, families raised and one suddenly finds themselves faced with their own reflection in a void of aspirations. Whatever the timing of our higher calling, it always comes with a receding of the noise and busy-ness of life, or at least a dire need for that receded, breathing space. In this space, self can finally meet self in a more authentic way. It is in the quiet spaces between the moments that we can hear the voice calling us to something more, to a higher path. Sadly, not everyone allows themselves to hear or answer their calling, and few learn to partner with the source of that calling.

What does this all mean? If we ponder on it for a moment, the idea of a calling means there is something outside of the confines of our individual lives doing the calling. As we sense this calling, there is an interaction between us and the source of the calling. Something other than us knows which way our life should ideally go, and is calling us to that destiny. We can then choose to heed and answer this call, or not. The existence of a calling to our life's purpose automatically assumes the existence of a greater plan or design, which *we* do not yet know. But something else knows. Both notions of life calling and life purpose directly place our individual existence within the context of something greater, our lives fulfilling a function like threads in a large existential tapestry. And for such a call and answer interaction, for guidance to occur, we must surely acknowledge the existence of a sentient intelligent force, which exists beyond us. Sensing and responding to that something as it calls to us from behind veils means that this intelligence has greater horizons and insights than we do: it knows what we do not yet know. From my experience and observation, I see this larger intelligence constantly seeking to partner with us all, to help along the journey towards a desirable evolutionary destiny. It is up to us whether we partner with it or not. Like everything in life, whatever we choose will set in motion its consequential outcomes.

What is this invisible force calling to us? What is this ineffable whisper in our hearts, asking unspoken questions for the answers we need? This book is my attempt to share of my understanding. I write from my personal experience and current level of knowing, as well as what I learnt from other Souls who have, like me, spent lifetimes exploring this question and its answers. Out of these explorations has come an awareness of the importance of consciously embracing a partnership with this transcendent intelligence guiding our lives.

I am no one, and yet I am everyone who has travelled the spiritual path for a while and achieved some measure of success with it. I have been blessed to meet and learn from some great Souls along the way. I am far from perfect, yet I can honestly claim to have dedicated myself to consciously evolve and serve for a long time. Along the way, I made some bold intelligent choices, as well as some stupid ones, which just goes to show that we don't have to be perfect in order to grow and transform on the spiritual path. I have applied myself to personal discovery and spiritual development with ongoing commitment. I have gained a working knowledge and understanding of myself, of human nature, spiritual evolution, and the path of Personal Spiritual Alchemy. I have been blessed to be surrounded by some amazing Souls, who have shared their wisdom with me. This book is not an autobiography, nor is it an academic offering. I will not cite articles, classical alchemical works, or the sacred texts from the rainbow of spiritual traditions this world has produced. Anyone wishing to inquire into and cross-reference the insights shared in this book with those of the Wise Ones who have come before are welcome to do so on their own. I share what I learnt, feel, know and can access at this point in my soul journey. It is then up to you to feel, with an honest heart and an open mind, whether what I share resonates with the deeper truth felt within your Soul's Knowing, and within the Mind of God.

The lives of those who travel the spiritual path all follow similar grand patterns and key stages. The wise learn from their experience; the wisest also learn from other people's experience. I already share the fruits of my evolutionary labours and study with my students. Here I simply translate into words the Knowing I have been privileged to receive. I hope this to be of benefit to you, and perhaps it will save you a bit of time on your own journey. If you're interested in exploring with me, then welcome my friend!

The Illusion of Separateness

I have often joked that my middle-age crisis happened at 15, imploding on that snowy night on my window ledge. While my life crisis did not involve the purchase of a fast sports car or a radical change of career (I was a bit too young for either!), it involved a drastic realignment of my aspirations and life direction. It was the night I made the crossroad decision to stop being a passenger in my *normal* life, and actively answer the call from Soul. The best part of my story began with my awakening to the great benevolent guiding force who is present, in unique yet similar ways, in all our lives.

Most people in our modern mechanised world fancy themselves to be separate, individual creatures, with absolute free-will and the limitless autonomy to do whatever they want, whenever they want, however they want. It's funny how they often begrudge the consequences! Anyone throughout history who has attained to respectable levels of genuine wisdom and enlightenment will clearly tell you: this reality of separateness and endless free-will is a fallacy. It is the limitations of third-dimensional reality which completely convince people they are nothing but their body-mind. Trapped by the perception of their physical senses, they believe and feel themselves to be only their physical body, emotional nature, and intellectual self. Relatively rare are the individuals who can genuinely know and experience themselves beyond the glass-ceiling of the body-mind to glimpse their eternal spiritual nature.

These more spiritually developed humans feel and know themselves to be the animating Soul, currently embodied in this human form. Such Soul-identified individuals know they have a body-mind, yet they know they are not their body-mind; they are the conscious presence and energy animating their human form. In other words, they are a spiritual being having a human experience, rather than the reverse. While we are all be familiar with the concept of Soul, a relative few of us actually know ourselves to be the Soul. Even language betrays our human lack of first-hand experience of Soul identification. How often do you hear people say "I have a soul", when in fact the reverse is true: it is the Soul that has you!

A human being can be spiritually asleep, or in fluctuating degrees of being spiritually awake. A human being who identifies as their body-mind invests solely in material, emotional, social, and intellectual activities. These domains of activity and interaction address, stimulate, nurture and feed every part of the being he or she considers themselves to be. Please do not think that I consider such aspects of human life unimportant; it is immensely necessary to the nurture the evolution and growth of the human entity on every level. No matter how spiritual we are, all aspects of our human-ness are part of our spiritual journey. Walking the talk of the spiritual path in an integrated way means healing, purifying and spiritualising ourselves from the ground up, and beyond. Only by tending to the health and development of every level of our being — physical, emotional, mental, social and spiritual - can we foster the achievement of our greatest potential. This integrated approach to spiritual growth contributes evolutionary value not only to ourselves, but also to the collective learning and evolution of humanity. Only the wisdom and light we ground and actualise into our human vehicle can take root in the earth plane, and be shared with the world.

Certain spiritual traditions and practitioners have held judgment of the embodied aspect of human experience, making the "flesh" element of our existence almost evil, the enemy of spiritual enlightenment. Grounded aspects of our humanity have too often been demonized, set in opposition to the world of Spirit. This has given rise to a common impulse to escape the messiness of human living, striving to bliss out in some heavenly realm far removed from our daily difficulties. This is a sad lack of acknowledgement of the miracle of earth life itself. We must not forget that Spirit is present in all things, even down to the biological level. The escapist, bliss-bunny approach to spirituality is also a cowardly way to approach one's spiritual growth. Most issues the spiritual aspirant faces exist in the all-too-human levels of the self. It is too easy to throw it all in the too-hard basket and abandon ourselves by pretending it's not there. To judge or deny our grounded humanity and its imperfections is an act of sidestepping our issues, instead of addressing them. The higher realms are blissful and amazing, but also unattainable to maintain unless we make our human selves clear vessels for the anchoring of Spirit. The key to permanently integrating and grounding expanded states of being - often referred to as enlightenment- is to face and clear the fear, separation consciousness and baggage in both the human self and the embodied Soul experience. Embracing the mirror of lessons and challenges that Earth life offers is key to success on the spiritual path.

It is true, admittedly, that anyone seriously seeking the attainment of spiritual enlightenment and God actualisation will, at different times in their journey, need to withdraw from the hustle and bustle of human activity. Everyone, in some phases of their evolutionary Soul journey, will need to retire to their metaphorical "cave" and make time to focus on soul-searching, deeper states of being and communing with the beyond. This, however, occurs at key times in a soul's journey and only for finite periods of time. Such cave-times are akin to that of creating a cocoon which will nurture the transformation of the evolving Soul. Once the transformation is complete, the spiritual disciple goes back into the world to express and share of his newfound love, wisdom, and light. Only by demonstrating mastery of self among the challenges of the concrete world, and sharing of what we have learnt, can we truly actualise our growth. Love is meant to be shared, not selfishly hogged, and there is no mastery in avoiding the things that challenge us to be better. In order to be productive of genuine spiritual transformation, our periods of retreat from the world should never be motivated by fear or judgment of the human experience. To run away in disgust is a choice of fear, not one of love. Spirit, God, the Universe - whichever you wish to call it -abides within All. To push away and reject our humanity as un-spiritual reveals an inner contradiction and blindness to the presence of Spirit within All. It makes no sense to say "God is All", only to reject part of Creation as "not part of God" because we have issues with it. It is also hypocritical and very miserly to access greater realms of universal love in meditation, only to withhold that love from our whole selves, or from our sphere of influence.

There is another side of the coin to this, however; there always is in spiritual matters. The other side of this truth is that there are many human attitudes and activities, and many aspects of our human world, which are mutually exclusive to the achievement of true enlightenment and God realisation. Things like indulging in destructive behaviours, addiction, being mean-spirited, cruel, selfish, arrogant, tyrannical or consumed by lust are experiences which pull us closer to our fear-based animal nature, and further away from our divine nature. This is not because those things are not part of God, or of Creation; nor does it mean we should fear or judge them. It is simply that those things cause devolution rather than evolution. It's like driving in the wrong direction on a freeway; it's bound to cause problems. The patterns of Universal evolution expect an animal to function guided by fear and instinct, but expect human beings to behave according to more evolved motives and intentions. Choosing to give into fearful, self-preserving animalistic behaviour is going backwards in evolution. So while we must not judge or deny the imperfections of our humanity, we must train, harness and refine our human nature towards its purest and truest nature. If we orient ourselves towards this goal, we will eventually progress to the point of hearing a call from our Divine parent. With some realignment, we will begin to perceive the great invisible hand which always and in all ways encourages us up the evolutionary spiral, as any wise parent would guide their children. Like any journey, we begin from right where we are and progress, one step after another, towards our ultimate destination. For the unconscious human, believing themselves to be only the body-mind in a third-dimensional world, the first step is to become a good, civilised and moral human. The next step is to seek that which lies beyond the forms of concrete existence. The first port of call in this spiritual search, the first whisper to call out to the spiritual seeker, is not the ultimate big guy- God- but the level of God closest to us, the tree which gives us life: our Soul Tree.

Call and Answer: A bridge towards the Divine

The initial experience of a calling towards "something more" than third-dimensional existence is the first response from Soul towards the human seeking to connect with their ineffable nature. Regardless of your story, this calling happens because you, as a human being, have been searching, asking, and are now ready to make a connection. On the other side of the veil, the Soul of which you are an expression wants to connect too. It wants to claim the human "you" to become an earthly vehicle through which the Soul can experience earth life, evolve and love. It is, therefore, a two-way extension between the human creature and Soul. Both aspects then establish a connection, with a view to merge and become integrated as we grow. This is the beginning of the path of spiritual initiation: each major transformation is a step towards merging and integrating with the Soul.

Understand one thing: It is the soul who directs the journey of reconnection and merging between human and Soul, not the human. There is an order to the Universe. The higher levels of Creation are the boss, and dictate to the lower levels of Creation. The lower levels of Creation are meant to serve the will and purpose of the Higher Intelligences of Life, which we are a small part of. As above, so below. In the same way, the higher levels of self are the boss of little you. In order for this soul-to-human bridging to occur, you must shape yourself to fit the Soul, not the other way around. There is much humility necessary for the spiritual aspirant to remember their individual place in the pecking order of Creation. The Calling is in truth a response to your searching and readiness, but make no mistake: you are there to take instruction, not make demands.

Many people confuse this initial calling back to the spiritual self with a call from the ultimate God of All. Yet, the calling is from the next step up the Divine ladder. Of course, you could say it is all God in the end, but there are degrees and levels of "God-ness". As I have said before, there is an order to the Universe and Creation. A human creature who is just experiencing the first stirrings of spiritual awakening does not get to go straight to the big boss, dealing directly with the very Source of All Creation, Time, Space, Infinity and Forever! To expect so is a little arrogant. It would be like a high-school student applying for their first job in their local Dunkin' Donut shop expecting their recruitment interview to be a one-on-one with the CEO of the whole multinational company. Lacking in humility much?

Instead, like any other creature evolving through the spiritual ranks, you get your first spiritual contact with the next level up above you in the Spiritual Tree of Life. From then on, you embark upon a wondrous journey and work your way up the evolutionary spiral.

For me, the call came early, and it came loudly. So loudly in fact that considering any other life path filled me with despair and despondency. Confining myself solely to the realm of the body-mind and its concrete existence was not a life I considered worth living. So I had a choice: Give up, or answer the call.

Evolution Is Not Optional: The Two Paths of Planetary Initiation

Regardless of the unique phenomena of your experience, all human beings share a common thread of existence: we are all on a path of evolution. Few engage with the process consciously, but evolution is the very impulse of life. No one and nothing that exists escapes it. Nothing is static, everything changes all the time. Everything evolves: plants, animals, people, planets, empires, ideas and ideologies... Darwin made the case for biological evolution, but of course the same applies to other levels of our existence. Change is the only constant in life, and our primary responsibility in life as sentient beings is to evolve. How can we do this? Thankfully, we are not alone nor without support. Those who open their hearts and minds to it can discern an invisible benevolent intelligence guiding this evolutionary process at all levels of Creation. It comes to us through the Calling to a higher life path. It talks to us through the deep, quiet whispers within our hearts. It counsels us through our conscience. It reveals itself to us through the stirrings of the Soul and its timeless, deeper currents of feeling. It guides us through a higher sense of intuition. It reveals itself in a myriad of ways to the seeker who gets out of their own way enough to perceive this ineffable Benevolence.

Many spiritual practices, from mindfulness to meditation and prayer, aim to discipline the human mind and emotions so that one may hear the voice of Spirit. Much of what we call spiritual guidance comes in fact from our Soul Tree. Some will be the work of beings existing on higher planes and tasked with assisting the evolution of humanity. Further guidance comes from the intelligence of various aspects of life processes, for instance in nature or on a larger planetary level such as the Earth Mother. We indeed have plenty of support! Be discerning, however: not all guidance from the invisible realms is good or even benevolent. Disembodied souls -the souls of those who have passed- are an example. The soul of the restless, those with unresolved issues or who met a traumatic end, sometimes linger in their astral forms rather than move on to the next phase of their journey after death. Contrary to some beliefs, dying doesn't instantly make you wise or enlightened. If you were an idiot when you were alive, you'll still be an idiot after you die. Talking to the dead gives you as good a chance of receiving enlightened advice as you would get from random people on the street. I would not advise it, if what you seek is higher wisdom and clarity. You must therefore attune your spiritual ear like you would tune a radio to receive the frequencies of a particular radio station, and not others. Through your intention and personal boundaries, choose to only align and attune only to the guidance which comes from higher planes of unconditional love, light and truth, and which serves your highest good. Aim your mental receiver into higher planes and vibrations of unconditional love and light, and hold clear boundaries about what you allow yourself to receive and be guided by.

Beyond the invisible guiding force of the Soul Tree and the unseen realms, grounded help exists in the form of embodied spiritual teachers, as well as the religions and spiritual traditions of this world. These agents of Spirit can provide a bridge, and pass on useful skills and wisdom to those seeking to climb their way up the Soul Tree and back to Source.

There are currently two official paths of spiritual progression on this planet: the Religious Path (also called the Path of Saviourship) and the Path of Personal Spiritual Alchemy (also called the Path of Transformation through Mastery). For most of the history of this planet, the Path of Religion has been the only officially sanctioned path of spiritual initiation. The teachings of Spiritual Alchemy are very ancient indeed, but Personal Spiritual Alchemy was not recognised as an official path of planetary initiation until recently, at the dawning of the Age of Aquarius.

There are many current surviving religions of the world: from yogic traditions to Buddhism, Judaism and Christianity, Islam and more. Regardless of the religion that one may follow, they all include a similar design: initiation into becoming a member of said religion, observing specific rituals and practices, subscribing to a set of beliefs and stories, and adopting a code of moral rules to live by. The presence of these elements in all the religions of the world is not random. All religions, in their own way, include into their theory and practice the ingredients which aim to support to development of moral character, dedication to spiritual ideals and, in its most lofty expression, a selfless dedication to serving the greater good. There are many commonalities between the Path of Religion/Saviourship and the Path of Personal Spiritual Alchemy/Transformation through Mastery. Both seek to facilitate the evolving soul towards the same evolutionary goals: the refinement of one's character, the enlightenment of mind and heart, the progression of the soul through the process of spiritual initiation and transformation into a wise, loving soul expression dedicated to selfless spiritual service. Religion and spiritual alchemy differ mainly in the mechanisms utilised to facilitate such progression. Each path suit some souls better than others.

Religion works at a collective level through the mechanism of devotion. Followers relate to God, their Source, through their devotion to the intermediary of their religion's figurehead: The path to God is, in a way, "through Him", the Messiah. Religion gathers the various strata of its followers and encourages them to follow and live by the teachings of their faith, and to be devoted to the figurehead of that religion. The practice of living by a set of moral rules facilitates the civilising of their human nature, turning them into better versions of themselves in evolutionary terms. The devotion to an idealised Messiah figure also gradually shapes them in the image of their Messiah. All this, over time, prepares them for the major transitions of the various spiritual initiations. The crossing of the threshold of major planetary initiation requires, however, the removing of unresolved karma. Unresolved karma is the disharmonious baggage and evolutionary negative impacts created in the world through the past choices of fear made by each Soul as they journey, life after life, through time on this little planet. Each major spiritual initiation requires that the Soul be free of certain karmic encumbrances in order to step through the initiatory gateway. The Path of Saviourship relies on the figure of a Saviour, Messiah or World Teacher to cyclically incarnate and process the unresolved collective karma of the followers who have made themselves ready for initiation. All the disciples ready for a particular level of initiation go through the initiatory threshold, all together, as their Saviour removes their collective karmic impediments. When Christian followers say that Jesus took on their sins, they are being literal, and correct in a karmic sense. This is the religious mechanism for spiritual progression: adopting moral guidelines of living to refine one's character, be devoted to a Saviour in the image of whom you shape yourself, and allowing Him to save you from your own karma in order to progress to the next level of spiritual initiation. This approach means, however, that the progression of individual Souls has to wait until the Messiah comes, and everyone goes through together.

Progression on the Path of Personal Spiritual Alchemy relies on a different mechanism: insight into the Truth and the development of self-mastery. Personal Alchemy works more at the individual level, as pace of progression does not rely on the coming of a World Teacher, but on the individual soul's hard work in meeting key benchmarks of mastery of self. Anytime the student is ready, they can undergo initiation. Despite the individual pace of progress, this does not mean that group work is absent from this path. It is the way of things that anyone undergoing the process of spiritual initiation will work as part of a collective of like-minded souls at a similar level of progression. Alchemy, however, does not forever bind the disciple to a group, waiting for progression together at a time defined by the coming of a Saviour. Instead, it enables each individual disciple to move between different groups of other initiates based on their individual attainment. Like attracts like, therefore group connections are formed based on similarity of vibration, common purpose and shared reality. Alchemy is a merit-based system which brings fluidity to the soul's progression through the initiation process: if you work hard and do well, you can progress faster without having to wait for the others in your group, or for the coming of a great Soul. If you do badly or regress, however, the opposite can happen. Much support is given to anyone who struggles, but participation in initiate groups goes hand-in-hand with upholding key standards of clarity, purity, light, mastery, love and wisdom.

Another key difference between the Path of Saviourship and the path of Spiritual Alchemy is that Alchemy makes no use of Saviours to process karma, nor does it place permanent intermediaries between the evolving Soul and God. Each soul studies and practice at length the spiritual alchemical practices and tools that enable them to process their own karmic load. Since there is no karmic Saviour on this path, each disciple works hard to remove the karmic impediment to their own progression into the next level of initiation.

Disciples also develop, through practice and spiritual insight, a growing direct relationship with God by working their way up their Soul Tree (a process explained in more details in further chapters). I am often questioned as to why students of the Alchemical Path require a teacher, if indeed this approach places no intermediary between the student and God. Contrarily to religion, the alchemical Hierophant does not place themselves as "the way" through which the students connect to God. For a spiritually awakening person to reconnect to God with any real clarity, however, takes practice, correct alignment and attunement, purification, expansion of consciousness and time. There are many pitfalls on the way, and no one can do it alone. Evolution is like a chain, where those a few steps ahead assist those a few steps behind. No junior initiate has a direct and immediate line to the Great Creator of All. All souls can, however, gradually enter into the Mind of God in their own right as they progress up the evolutionary ladder of initiation. A good Teacher on the path of Alchemy will teach you how to do this for yourself, while supporting you with their own wisdom and energy in the meantime. The end goal is always to help you establish and strengthen your own direct connection to the Divine, but offering a temporary leg up and feedback mirror in the meantime. Like anything else in life, new skills must be learnt. If you wish to become a great piano player, you are likely to need to take lessons from a piano teacher. If you wish to become a Master, you must take instruction from a Master, or at least an impressive Teacher who is a few steps ahead of you in their evolution, and can pass on what they know. More on this topic in Chapter 5. This is and has ever been the way of spiritual progression: we are all but links in a lineage of ancient wisdom which gets passed on from teacher to student, and on, and on...

Both the Path of Saviourship and the Path of Personal Spiritual Alchemy require the evolving soul to meet to same criteria of pure heart, pure character, self-control, love, selflessness and other such wonderful qualities in order to complete the stages of spiritual initiation. Each path, however, goes about it differently. In summary, the Path of Saviourship relies on the progression of the whole collective of followers of a religion at once, through the intercession of a Saviour.

The Path of Spiritual Alchemy allows for more individually timed progression fuelled by personal insight and the hard work of the individual disciple to clear the way for themselves. Religion is more gradual and offers a wonderful experience of belonging with one's group, as everyone journeys together. Alchemy, although still including group work, emphasises personal karmic responsibility and allows faster progression for those with the confront and courage to embrace the process.

There is no better or worse path. Those in the early stages of spiritual awakening and the early initiations are often better served by the Path of Religion. After that, it is a matter of personal choice. Once a spiritual initiate achieves into the higher levels of planetary initiation, they tend to move into a model of Transformation through Mastery, because there comes a time when a junior spiritual Master must no longer rely on a Saviour to progress, but must save themselves based on their own spiritual hard work instead.

As you would have guessed, this book explores the process of spiritual evolution and initiation from the angle of the Path of Personal Spiritual Alchemy. I do not claim it is the only way, or the best way. The Path of Transformation through Mastery is not suited to everyone, nor is everyone suited to it. Like almost everyone, my Soul journey followed the Path of Religion over many lifetimes on this beautiful little planet. In more recent times, guided by my Soul Tree, I came to seeking the next step in my spiritual travels. The path of Personal Spiritual Alchemy found me and I found it. We fit together snug and lovely. A lifetime of study in this field of spiritual progression has so far been both extremely challenging and immensely rewarding. I have grown and progressed in ways I never even imagined. It is indeed from my own experiences, hard work, study, and revelations that I draw and share the contents of this book, combined with the wisdom shared by some of the great Souls I have known along the way.

CHAPTER 2

The Tree of Life and The Soul Tree

~~~

Every single person is on a journey of spiritual evolution, whether they know it or not. Every life has a purpose, big or small. Many receive a calling towards a life path, which must serve the soul's learning and evolution. Some listen and follow the call, some remain blind to it, caught up in the world of egoic unconsciousness. Some are ready to receive a calling towards reunification with their Soul and the Soul Tree, and a relative few receive the call to fulfil a purpose in service to something greater than themselves. For those who are ready, Soul and human reach towards each other in a way which produces spiritual reawakening and a call to the spiritual path. What does it mean to be "ready"? And ready for what? For the pieces of this puzzle to fall into place, I need to explain the mechanics of spiritual evolution and initiation. But in order to do this, I must place the information within the context of how Creation works. So yes, we are starting right at the beginning of everything…

Basics of Spiritual Cosmology

We are an integral part of a great creational Universe. The Tree of Life models of various cultures and traditions are simply an attempt at conceptualising the structure of Creation: Its aspects, streams, planes and dimensions.

'As above, so below' is a well-known hermetic axiom which refers to the existence of patterns within Creation. These patterns repeat over and over, on various levels of the Universe: from the highest and most expanded levels down to the tiniest creatures. The same laws, principles and divine architectural essence govern all Life at every level of our Universe; they simply express on a different scale, scope and level of complexity. In order to understand ourselves, we must therefore understand the Universe that we form a part of. Reversely, we can find a path of insight into the workings of the Universe by truly knowing ourselves in meaningful ways. Interestingly, "Know Thyself" is another ancient hermetic spiritual axiom, and it's not a coincidence! Hermeticism is an ancient body of occult theory passed down through the ages since (very) ancient Egyptian times, which exposes some of the foundational principles of Spiritual Alchemy.

Every creature on Earth evolves. Creation is in a constant dance of change, slowly, over an eternity of time, and beyond what we conceptualise as time. This Creational Universe is intelligent and trends towards the exploration of what it can be, what it can do, what it can become and towards the realisation of its amazing potential. We are in major meaning-of-life territory here, as I basically stated in one sentence a very simplified answer to existential questions like 'What's the point of it all?" or "Why do we exist?".

As with most spiritual truths, the answer bears a simplicity which betrays its profoundness. Bear in mind that any verbal explanation about mysteries like why Creation exists, or what the point of it is, will be doomed to represent a limited understanding. Such big questions probe into levels of existence clearly beyond our little monkey mind's ability to grasp. Throughout our collective history, a few amazing individuals managed to evolve spiritually to such enlightenment and expansion of consciousness that they could, in a slightly less limited way than most humans, grasp some of the bigger picture of what Life is about. They passed on their insights and wisdom to their students, and again and again from Master to student over the centuries. This ancient wisdom endured as best as it could, kept alive by the Wisdom Keepers of various ancient lineages. Sadly, much of it was also lost, distorted or destroyed along the way. Religions have attempted to convey some of the Ancient Wisdom too, each with their own cultural flavour and within the particular historical and political context of the era which birthed them. Human struggles for power and domination, however, caused conflict between religions, traditions and cultures, leading to the destruction of some of our Timeless Wisdom. Sources of wisdom are not all lost to history however; even in our modern, mechanistic era, some rare souls live and have explored in their own right. Though few they are, they have themselves contributed to the body of eternal spiritual wisdom available to the human race.

What has come out of such cosmic explorations by the great Master Souls and advanced mystics of Earth, past and present, is that God/the Universe/Source seeks to know Itself through the manifestation and experience of its own Creation. Source, or God, is exploring Its own nature, Its own potential as to what It can be, can create, become, learn, and evolve into. One could say our very existence is part of a grand Cosmic journey of Self-exploration and growth by our Divine Source.

As above, so below… We see a scaled up and scaled-down version of the same pattern through Creation: our own existential purpose is also, at our own level, to have experience, learn from it, grow and evolve into more of our potential. Our evolutionary journey is a micro correspondence of the process that Creation itself –

God - undergoes. Yet our own purpose goes further than simply being a correspondence of the Higher Purpose: our own evolutionary explorations are not detached from the big game, they contribute to it. We are an intrinsic part of Source and its Creation. We exist *because* we are a part and an expression of Source. We are literally tendrils of the Source of All Life, extended into realms of matter and currently having a human experience on planet Earth. As we evolve, our learning is part of the learning of All That Is. When we truly learn our Soul lessons, upload them to become part of who we are and what we are becoming, we contribute our little bits of learning and evolution to the greater Evolution of All That Is. In other words, the point of life is to explore, have experiences, learn from them and as a result evolve to become a version of ourselves which is closest to our Divine potential. As we reach closer to our most expansive and amazing potential, we contribute this achievement to our Source, and help Creation achieve the same. In this sense, one might say that our primary directive and reason for being is to evolve so that God can realise Its potential, through Its Creation. Evolution therefore means becoming a more complete expression of one's expansive Divine potential.

According to almost every myth or even modern Science, at the beginning, there was either nothing or a sort of infinity. I must clarity here that the term 'beginning' in itself places a limitation upon a Cosmic creational process which may truly be infinite, though the human mind struggles to grasp the concept. The "beginning" referred to here would be the beginning of our Creational Universe, or perhaps the beginning of this current incarnation of Creation. What if all of Creation itself was but one day in the Cosmic Journey? One life in the Soul journey of our Source? The logical human mind cannot fully grasp such realities, but only approach them conceptually. The eternal truths lying beyond our Creation are perhaps beyond our current human capability to know with any certainty. Yet, the clear mind enlightened by Divine Illumination and assisted by an expansion of consciousness can perceive some of the mysteries, in part at least. Though the logical mind cannot know beyond the concrete world, the enlightened mind informed by an expanded consciousness knows that nothing (or the Void) and infinity are two sides of the same coin, or perhaps two ways to look at the same thing. Within a Source Universe, nothing is never just nothing. The Void is simply potential yet un-manifest: it has no form and no expression, yet within it exists all potential for all things. The Void of the original nothingness is like a cauldron filled with the invisible potion from which All Life can be created. In other words, it is the womb of Creation into which the sparks of Life must ignite and set all creative impulses into motion.

At some point beyond space and time as we know it, and by some miracle not fully within our understanding, there was a beginning to this Creation. As far as some scientists and spiritual mystics can tell, this was both an implosion and an explosion within the nothingness that was before. Our Unified Source both imploded itself into two aspects of itself – namely the Void and the spark Fire of Life - and then big-bang exploded itself into existence through the Cosmic copulation of the two. These two aspects of the original One Source are often defined as one being Feminine or receptive (the Void womb, Goddess), and one being Masculine or transmitting in nature (the Life fire or Spark, God). This motif is found in the common Tree of Life models of occult cosmology, be it the as part of the Jewish mysticism tradition of the Kabbalah, or within the Khemitic (or Hermetic) tradition of pre-dynastic

Ancient Egypt. As above, so below... The way human beings reproduce is, as we know, a similar process on a much smaller level, on the physical material plane of existence: The woman's womb and egg, seemingly empty of any baby yet brimming with creative potential, awaits to receive the dynamic impulse of the man's seed. From here, conception occurs and a cascade of miraculous life processes and divisions turns these original little seeds into a manifest and complex human being. The miracle of the creation of life happens all around us all the time, on small scales and big scales: humans, animals, plants, as well as stars, solar systems and galaxies. The expression and appearance may be different, but the essence and principle are always the same. Patterns repeat. We can learn much if we just stop, observe with the eyes of our heart, commune and wonder at the miracle of it all.

Anyone who has achieved success in life will know that good relationships are necessary for anything to thrive. Our ability to achieve inner peace and good self-esteem is anchored in the quality of our relationship with ourselves. Successful business and trade are founded on mutually beneficial relationships. Family relies on ordered, loving relationships. Growing food involves many levels of relationships between humans, the land, plants, the sun and water. Good health requires a healthy and balanced relationship between the needs of our bodies and our external lifestyle and environments. Genuine artistic or scientific creativity requires a relationship between the heart and the mind, between the ability to reach into intuitive levels of inspiration and the practical ability to engineer or manifest them into physical reality. Any learning requires us to relate with someone or something else: a new topic, a new perspective, a new experience or a new teacher. Everything that is created, innovated, nurtured and thriving relies on one thing relating to another, nourished by love (whether it is the love of the other person, the love of an idea or the love of money!). This is simply how life works: nothing really exists in isolation. Everything comes out of the interaction of at least two elements, with love connecting us and nurturing the Life within all things produced from this interaction. As above, so below…. We can therefore infer that the core importance of relationships in creative and life-nurturing endeavours must be a pattern of design on a greater level. This interrelatedness and interdependence of All Life trickles down to us through the amazing fractal perfection of the Divine Creational pattern.

At the beginning, Unified Source imploded into two parts of itself so that each aspect- Masculine-Transmitting and Feminine-Receptive- could interact and relate with each other to manifest Creation. Just like human reproduction, communication or electrical circuits, Creation requires transmitting and receptive polarities to establish a feedback loop between each other in order enable the circuitry to exchange energy and create something. We are part of this web of Life loops as much as any other creature.

From the original interaction between transmitting God-Force and receptive God-Source, the beginnings of Creation sprung forth. The Big Bang banged, God spoke 'The Word', emitted the initial vibration, the primordial sound which began setting into motion the cascade of miraculous processes which manifest all into existence. As this primary unified wave of Divine vibration began radiating, it aspected itself into 12 Cosmic Rays. These twelve resounding Divine notes continued on and evolved, emitting more vibrations and weaving those vibrations into patterns, rhythms and structures. Creation was slowly weaving itself into being. These Divine patterns, rhythms and structures of Creation are the truth behind the meaningfulness of sacred geometry, mathematics, and all the sciences, as well as the arts. Just like at human conception, Divine Creation involved a process of subdivision and gradual architecture of its raw materials. As it expanded, the creational emanation continued to divide itself into more parts, enabling more relationships, weaving and interactions between these parts of Itself.

This expanding, interwoven, complex tapestry of Divine relationships enables more potentials and possibilities for Creation to discover, create and be. By exploring the vastness of All that It can be, and creating through the interactions of its parts, Original Source can grow, thrive, learn and experience Itself. We are absolutely woven within the very fabric of this Divine exploration. As it continued to subdivide, Source vibration morphed into more concrete form expressions, and structured itself into a number of planes and dimensions, each featuring particular manifestations and qualities of experience.

As the great Creational process continued, Source wanted to experience Its own Creation, and so Source emanated an infinite number of Monads, which divided into Oversouls, and Soul Groups and Soul Extensions, in the same way that a Tree branches out into separate main branches, small branches and individual leaves. These Monads and their Soul Extensions exist to inhabit and experience the realms of planes and dimensions, but were created without real awareness of their nature or Cosmic origins. We, creatures, are the physical expression of these Souls, like leaves at the end of branches on a Soul Tree. We will explore the concept of Soul Tree and Monad in more details later in this chapter. For now, we are simply getting our bearings regarding where we exist within this great Web of Life which is our Creation. We, as embodied human Souls, are the end of a long chain of subdivision of Source energy, designed to experience the various levels, worlds and qualities of the structure of Creation. The Oversoul is our Soul Tree, the Monad is like our Soul Forest, which is in turn part of a greater Monadic cluster, and beyond, all the way back to Source like a fractal pattern of Itself.

Out we emanated and manifested from the Source of All Life, to go forth, experience, learn and evolve. Life expands as it explores Itself and grows. One day, we will go back and return our Knowing all the way to our spiritual home, closing the loop between us and Unified Source, thereby ending this Cosmic Day's adventures. This is, ultimately, the great journey of Creation and evolution. In Hinduism, this great Cosmic loop is called the Cycle of Brahma: a repeating cycle of creation-emanation and reabsorption-ending. All that is created and emanated must then be gathered back home and end, only to be renewed in order to do it all again on a different turn of the Divine Spiral. Each loop is only one turn on the seemingly infinite reincarnation spiral of Divine Life.

The Rhythm of Life

Ancient wisdom and the simple observation of nature make apparent the cyclic ebb-and-flow rhythm of Life. Plants and creatures are born, grow and then die, to be recycled in the earth and reborn again in a different form. On a Divine level, this manifests as the cyclic rhythms of out-breaths and in-breaths of God. The out-breath refers to the act of Source creating and emanating Creation, streaming and dividing its infinite essence into increasingly finite elements, and expanding its experience and Knowing.

Creation includes the creature levels of life which manifest on the physical, etheric, astral and mental planes. We are all more than familiar with the creature realm. Yet Creation also includes many other life streams and consciousness aspects existing on a multitude of planes of existence. This includes the angelic realms, the Elohim streams and other disembodied beings and intelligences which fulfil the various functions of the creational Universe. The complex cosmology of this is beyond the scope of this book. Let us simply say that the commonly held belief that we, Earth humankind, are the only form of intelligent sentient life in the universe is ludicrous. While some may debate the statement that humanity is an intelligent life form at all, we can at least state with some degree of deductive certainty that the Universe is anything but empty of sentient and intelligent life. Life exists in a myriad of forms and expressions, not just physical or biological. As long as Earth humans search only for that which is in their physical image, they will be blind to the many faces of Life. But I digress…

Back to our little cosmological lesson on the in-breath and out-breath of God. A simple metaphor for the divine out-breath season is that of a grand Cosmic spring. The seeds of life resting in the dark womb of winter suddenly sprout, throw out new green branches and leaves, and bloom into its many unique and diverse wonders. As the season expands into summer, branches grow larger and stronger and flowers turn to fruit. In cosmic summer, all the little aspects of Creation grow and bloom into their greater potential through their exploration, experience and garnered wisdom. But summer can't last forever, and autumn must come.

The in-breath season of the divine cycle, like our autumn, represents the phase of Source pulling itself back together in order to harvest its experience and wisdom into Itself, and integrate it as fertile soil for the next cycle. All the exploration, learning and evolution which has been achieved in that Cosmic cycle is slowly harvested and brought back home, to its original Source. Then comes the winter, where the blooms, leaves and fruits of summer are either eaten or composted, thereby reused and renewed to feed the next life cycle. The cosmic winter will be the end of this Creation, and the beginning of the transition into the next. Please bear in mind that we are dealing with unfathomable large amounts of time, so don't panic about *the end....* It's a long way off yet! On a Cosmic Creation level, we are still in the out-breath phase, which is why Creation and Knowing are still expanding. Our evolution from self-limited individual creatures to more expanded multi-dimensional beings is part of the exploratory expansion of our Cosmos. Contracting and burying our consciousness in separation goes against the currents of our Creation's out-breath, and is therefore disharmonious and problematic. Evolution, expansion and growth are the order of this Cosmic day!

As above, so below... Just as these in-breaths and out-breaths seasons play out on the Divine Creation level, so do they exist at every other level of Creation. We know about the seasons, but our planet also has her creational cycles of out-breath and in-breath, as does our solar system, our galaxy and our universe. We exist within a dance of cycles, within cycles, within cycles. New solar systems and galaxies are born right now, and others are dying right now. Within the overarching Divine cosmic dance of in-breath and out-breath, every part of it also has its own life cycle, and not all of them happen at the same time. As biological humans, we know we follow the same pattern. Less known is the fact that the same applies to us as souls, and to our Soul Trees, Monad-Forests and beyond. Over eons of time, a Monad will come into manifestation from Source, and will in turn spawn Oversouls, which in turn will spawn Soul Extensions. Each Soul Extension will manifest a large number of embodiments into the creature levels. This is the out-breath of the Soul Tree creating and projecting out its life into the furthest reaches of matter. In time, the seasons turn and autumn comes with the spiritual imperative to harvest the garnered wisdom of the souls' experience. Every single soul has its own seasons, as do each Soul Tree and each Monad. How long this process takes, we don't know, but it is a very, very, very long time.

The spiritual calling comes to an embodied Soul as part of the process of continued expansion and growth in the life of the Monad. It is an invitation to more consciously participate in the great Monadic out-breath adventure. This is spiritual awakening, expansion of consciousness and Ascension, and it is not a fast process. Stepping onto the spiritual path is just a beginning in a very long journey of exploration of the possibilities of what the Monad can know, remember and learn of Itself. Our spiritual awakening is a beginning, and it is also an end. Awakening to our spiritual nature marks the end of a phase of existence as a separate unconscious leaf on the Soul Tree, lost in experience which is not always constructive. It marks the transition into another phase of returning home to the already held Knowing of the Tree, as well as contributing to and participating in the expansion of that Knowing. This return to the Knowing is the Holy Grail transformation that all spiritual seekers yearn for, as they prepare to spend the next eons of time exploring and remembering their cosmic origins, and reunifying with the larger Being that they are a part of. This is a joyful and awe-inspiring process, as much as a natural one. To recognise our place within the web of Life, and to work in harmony with the in-breath and out-breath cycles of our own soul's evolution, are key to finding inner peace and becoming an agent of positive change and Divine harmony. As above, so below. As we return to existing in unified harmony with the greater Life Tree that we are a part of, the more we can manifest this harmony and radiance into our lives and environment.

Before we further explore the Soul Tree and Monad experience, I will expand a little upon the hermetic adage of "as above, so below", as there are some common misconceptions on this topic.

Used as a tool for learning about God, "As above, so below" means that by observing and learning from the natural world within us and around us, we can discern Divine Design and therefore learn about the workings of the great Divine Machine. Many spiritual aspirants, initiates, and masters have had moments of enlightenment and divine revelation while being in a contemplative, receptive state within themselves, and often while in nature. Most people with energetic sensitivity and a spiritual orientation would attest to a healing, spiritual and inspiring energy within nature. I feel no need to make an argument in favour of this statement. Those who cannot feel it have perhaps picked the wrong book! Spirit is within all things; all things are made of God-stuff. This harks back to the process of Source dividing itself and projecting out into un-manifest energies and manifest forms in order to explore itself towards its fullest potential. As such, when we observe something as small as our bodies' natural functioning and the life processes in the natural world, we are basically observing a part of Creation playing out its patterns. We thus observe Universal Law at play, as manifested on our particular plane of existence. Please note that I said 'a part of Creation' and made a point to specify that we observe universal law "as manifested on our particular plane of existence". This is an important distinction because our little corner of Creation gives us the opportunity to study only a small sample of all that Creation has to offer. The patterns of life repeat in a fractal manner, in a spiral of decreasing scale; yet the parts do not contain the entirety of whole. The mistake made by the uninitiated is that of taking 'As above, so below', and extrapolating it to equally mean "As below, so above". But the two are not interchangeable! This is a distortion which has historically led human beings to project their own frailties onto the Divine. If one truly understands the process of Divine division, then one realises that every part of God-Source which has projected itself into form is but a small and often incomplete part of the whole. The deeper into manifested physical form a stream of God goes, the more division occurs along the way. The more division occurs, the smaller and more limited the end expression will be. It's simple maths. Observing ourselves or nature provides us with a template and a certain amount of insight into the workings of Creation itself, but is only an entry point into the mysteries of Life. One should not be too literal in copy-pasting what they observe and projecting it onto the Great Divine. To say Man was created in God's image is accurate. All of Creation was, in fact, created in God's image. This includes your dog and the tree in your garden… so perhaps God is actually Dog??... Bad jokes aside, confusing "As above, so below" with "As below, so above" has led humans to imagine a God who is in the image of Man! This is simply the projection of unenlightened minds trying to grasp the infinite. While the Whole is reflected in the smaller parts of itself, it is also so much greater than its individual parts. By saying "As below, so above", Man effectively projects its own limitations onto the Universe. This has created, among other things, the idea of a jealous, vengeful God. The metaphor I used earlier in this chapter to liken the great Cosmic in-breath and out-breath seasons with our earthly spring and autumn serve only to illustrate the ebb-and-flow pattern of Life. The simile bears some limitations however, as one cannot then make the literal leap of saying that 'divine fruits' actually grow in some heavenly garden, with farmer angels gathering the harvest at out-breath season! This would be a silly reductive, anthropomorphic projection. These metaphors are meant to illustrate underlying principles and the essence of a particular Knowing, not to be understood literally. To extrapolate from the lower towards the higher can only achieve one thing: impose our own limitations on that which is much greater and more complex than us.

In contrast, "As above, so below' tells us that Man realises he is a small part of a much larger Divine being, and exists by the Universal laws and patterns decreed by Source for all Creation. To return to a way of being and living which is in harmony with Divine design is the mandate of all evolving souls, including those who are incarnate but have forgotten what they truly are. What do I mean by this? How can souls forget who they truly are? Many Souls who project their energy all the way into matter experience a sort of material unconsciousness. The heresy of the five physical senses and of third-dimensional existence entomb soul consciousness in the illusion of separateness. The little leaves on the Soul Tree - the embodied soul-extensions - forget they are part of their Tree. They believe they exist independently of anything greater than them. This is the disconnection and spiritual sleep of egoic unconsciousness. Ego-identified creatures continue to experience their way through life, still supported to evolve, but they reality is disconnected from the Whole. They are still linked to their Soul, but the Soul drives the human being from a distance, like with a remote control. Human creatures begin the process of spiritually awakening only when they search for reconnection with something greater and more of themselves, beyond physical existence. The Soul answers the searching human. This is when a calling comes, the first of many calls to return home.

Spiritual awakening is a slow process, encompassing many stages. We were created in God's image, but forgot who we truly were along the way. Our task, if we wish to remember our true spiritual nature, is therefore to evolve to become more like God. As we reawaken and express our Divine Nature, we can become the embodied expression of it, walking in the world as the living realisation of the larger Being that we are a part of. This is what Spiritual Masters are and do. When we are steadfast in our practice of being more like God, a magical transformation happens: we are invited to partake, a little more, of the Mind of God. We experience the gradual purification of our character and the expansion of our consciousness. Our sense of who and what we are gradually unifies once again with Soul, our Soul Tree and beyond. This is the drawing-in process of coming back home, in spiritual terms. God divided itself into the various Monad, Soul Trees and Soul leaves; now the ascending human remembers itself to be at the end of the branch of their Tree so that they can bring awakening not only to themselves, but also to the world of matter. The more we realise and actualise the presence of the God within us while embodied in an unconscious world, the more we can ground and share the light of awakening into this world. This is how whole worlds evolve, through the collective evolution of its parts. As we bring the fruits of our evolution all the way into matter and grounded life, so we contribute to the awakening and evolution of the Earth. The expansion of our own out-breath cycle contributes to that of everything we touch and have an effect upon. Awakening is contagious!

This journey has many steps, the first of which is to reconnect with and be guided by the next level of "God" above us. This is the journey into Soul awakening, which then leads to the continued journey of expansion of consciousness into Oversoul, Monad, and beyond. This is the journey of partnering with our Soul Tree.

The Monad and the Tree of Life

The Tree of Life is a well-known symbolic model often used in myth, ancient cultures and religions to represent the structure and workings of Creation, and our place within it. Whether it is expressed as the Celtic Tree of life, with its branches and roots connecting to the wider circle of Creation, the Yggdrasil of Norse Mythology or the Tree of the Kabbala, the notion of a tree symbolises the layered complexity and interconnectedness of all Creation, its various levels, and its cyclic nature. Not being literal, we understand Creation is not made of actual trees in the earthly sense. Yet, it provides a useful metaphor for the subject at hand.

As part of springing forth into all the various expressions of life and experience, the energy from Source splits itself into smaller and smaller parts of itself. The Monads created in order to experience and inhabit the planes of form in Creation then also divides itself into smaller branches. In this way, this is akin to a tree: From its original seed and roots, a tree springs to life. From the central trunk come out major branches. Each main branch then splits into smaller branches, and as a final step, the small branches grow leaves. The pattern of growth, expansion and self-division that a tree follows is, in essence, a lower correspondence of how our Monadic and Soul trees manifest and divide from Unified Source. We, as human embodiments are the leaves at the end of the smallest Soul branches, also called Soul Extensions. We are the manifestation of the energy of the Soul Extension reaching into the levels of physical form life.

Why does the Monad do that? I would say it's two-fold: a vibrational necessity (Source possibly needs to divide itself in order to lower its vibration and enter more dense forms of expression), and diversity of experience and efficiency in covering as much ground as possible. Have you ever found yourself overwhelmed with a long to-do list and too little time to get to it all? Have you in those moments ever wished or said "If only I could have more of me! All these mini-me could be in different places at the same time and get this all done!" Well, the Monad *can* do that, and we are its mini-me's. Remember that the Monad is created without real memory or knowledge of its true nature or Cosmic origins. As such, the Monad is like a blank slate which allows infinite possibilities of exploration on behalf of Source, without pre-existing conditioning or the limits of previous choice or knowledge. We start from scratch and anything is possible. Just like Source, and on behalf of Source, the Monad logically seeks to experience, learn and grow to know Itself. What better way to do it than to spread out into as many varied expressions, forms, directions and modes as is possible? I am sure there are yet many modes, levels, planes, dimensions and expressions of Creation that even for the most advanced Master souls of this planet have not yet glimpsed. As far as is known, Source divides and expresses itself into three main life streams: The angelic life-stream who embody the processes of Creation, the Elohim life-stream who architect and engineer Creation, and the creature life-stream who experience Creation and learn to drive it. Each of these life-streams has their own Tree of Life structure, following the same fractal repeating patterns of Creation on ever-smaller scales. The creature life-stream is obviously what we are interested in since we, humans, belong to it.

What is a Monad, or a Soul Tree?

- It is one unit of Source energy, like a mini version of Source, after Source has split Itself into parts within the creature life-stream. The Monad has all the qualities and aspects of Source, but no real awareness of Its true nature or Divine origins, which is why the Monad seeks experience and learning, in order to know Itself. There is a very large number of Monads, a number appearing infinite to us. Relative to our metaphor of spiritual trees, the Monad would be what I call our Spirit Forest. From there, a few levels of subdivision occurs with every Monad, stepping down Its vibration at each step, and therefore manifesting in denser and denser levels of form at each level in the same way that Source originally did. As above, so below.... Patterns repeat.

- Following the pattern form Source, each Monad split into and manifests 12 Oversouls, which are the Soul Trees I have been referring to.

- Each Oversoul then subdivides into 12 Soul Groups, which would fit the analogy of being the major branches.

- Each Soul Group subsequently manifests 12 Soul Extension, which are like the personalities of the Soul Group, and are what we usually call the Soul. These are like the small branches from which leaves grow.

- Each Soul/Soul Extension can then manifest an almost infinite amount of embodiments, which are the leaves. These incarnations can happen anywhere in time or space. You, as the individual human person you know yourself to be, are just that: one embodiment, one ephemeral form expression within a limited chunk of space-time. You are one leaf, on one small branch of your Soul Group, which is in turn one branch of your Oversoul Soul Tree. The Oversoul itself is only one Soul Tree in your Monadic Forest, in a Creation that features an apparently infinite number of Monads.

(There is a fantastic YouTube video on this topic, called "The Basic Science of Ascension" by Michael King. It offers a visual of this process of Monadic subdivision and a summary of several points shared in this chapter and the next. See the last Chapter 7 for details of our YouTube Channel.)

Are you suddenly feeling a little small in a big universe? That's probably a good thing. A dose of existential humility is an important antidote to the illness of human ego rampant in our world: a world where everyone is being told they are special, where humans believe themselves to be the apex of evolution, top of the food chain, the only living creatures in the universe! From the higher perspective of higher beings and intelligences, the concept is laughable, since we are but the little leaves at the end of a branch of one tree in a vast cosmic forest. We have our part to play, but it is hard to take ourselves too seriously when we put our existence into perspective within the macrocosm of All That Is.

Another thing to remember is that we are but frail human creatures existing on a rock hurtling through space at incredible speed, within a small solar system, which itself is fast hurtling through a galaxy, which is itself hurtling through a universe and so on... Our obsession with needing control and certainty are again, seemingly ridiculous given the precariousness of our existence. We exist by the grace of a benevolent God-Goddess, truly. Should we be scared? No. How would that help anyway? There are many things out of our control in life. In truth, very few things are within our control. Living in terror of the things we cannot control is one of the most self-defeating behaviour I can think of. Instead, let us focus on doing our very best with the things which *are* within our control, and entrust the rest to the benevolence and intelligence of the Universal Mother, who – I think we can all agree – will be far wiser in the running of all Creation that we could ever be.

Our job is to be a good, healthy leaf which brings value to our Soul Tree. We need the Tree, but the Tree does not necessarily need us, especially if we prove more of a liability than an asset in evolutionary terms. The roots and trunk of a tree continue to nourish and provide the life-giving energy which keeps the branches and leaves alive. If the roots are pulled out, or if the trunk is damaged or sick, all the branches will also suffer and die. Yet one branch may grow sick and die, but the tree will continue on if it simply allows that branch to fall off. This is the universal order of things: We need Source to exist, but Source does not need each little individual creature in order to continue existing. Energy given can easily be withdrawn if the branch or leaf becomes sick and threatens the health of the entire tree.

The tree metaphor remains relevant for any Soul who becomes a problem child to the Tree over long periods of time. Just as a tree will allow a sick leaf or branch to die off and fall to protect the health of the tree, so the Soul Tree can withdraw its energy from the problem leaf, allowing it to fall off. This gives us another dose of humility medicine for the human sacred cow syndrome. We are created, loved and supported to evolve and contribute to our Soul Tree, and to Creation. But if we systematically refuse to play our part over long periods of time, misbehaving rather than working in step and harmony with what the Soul Tree requires of us, we become a source of illness and dis-ease to our Tree. We may become the leaf that is simply allowed to drop. Like all things in Creation, we have a purpose and a function.

Instead of trying to control the uncontrollable, let us focus on becoming the best, most useful leaves we can be.

Planes of Creation and the Spiritual Body System

There are many versions of the 'Tree of Life' model, which seek to define the structure and essence of Creation. I will provide a simple overview of my current understanding of the structure and quality of Creation, and how this expresses as the different levels of the human energy system. This entails the concept of planes and dimensions, which are terms often used interchangeably, but rarely truly understood.

As the Unified Source of all life implodes and explodes to manifest Creation, the energy released from this great act of cosmic birthing orders itself into particular structures and patterns of expression. Some energy remains purely energy, unfettered by the confining quality of form. Some energy takes form, descending into a denser, defined and "solid" way of expression. Please note here that the term 'form' does not signify just physical form. There are different levels of form life, each at varying levels of vibration and density. The denser the energy of life becomes, the more solid, heavy and concrete its expression. Physical form life is the densest expression of Source vibration within our realm, but there are other planes of form expression. Our physical eyes may not see other levels of form expression (although some people can), but it is still form.

As Source expands and lowers its vibration, it manifests layered degrees of increasingly structured and dense manifestation. Planes are the structural vibrational steps, or bandwidth levels, of form in Creation; a bit like notes in the music scale or floors in an apartment building. Each plane is a vibrational 'place' within which life forms from the human life-stream can exist and experience the particular quality and reality of that plane. Although we, as human being, experience physical life as the densest plane we inhabit, we also live within other planes of experience, such as the astral and mental planes.

Here is a quick overview of the levels and planes of our own human form self, which we continue to explore in this chapter:

- Physical: the concrete, experience of solid, liquid and gas; our physical body. This is considered the lower part of the physical body.

- Etheric: the etheric body is indelibly interwoven through our physical body and is usually considered the higher part of the physical body. It is the energetic blueprint and matrix for the physical body.

- Astral: This is the level of the emotional body, where we experience our emotional life.

- Mental: The mental body is where our thoughts, beliefs, intellects and other mental processes occur.

Each of these planes and associated bodies has a different density and heaviness. The physical is the hardest to move, change and slowest to adapt. The next step up in vibration is the astral plane; next is the mental plane. I am sure you can discern in your own personal experience the difference in density, resistance, inertia between your physical, emotional and mental experience. Ideas can come very fast, but it is comparatively slow to make them a reality in our physical life. Even the different speed between how fast we can think versus how fast we can write or talk highlights this difference in density and adaptability. In the same way, emotions can shift and change faster than our physical body (if we don't cling to them!). Our mind usually move quicker than our emotions; we can change how we think about something quicker than how we feel about it.

Next in the planes and bodies of our human energy system is what we term the 'higher planes' or higher bodies:

- Atmic
- Monadic
- Logoic
- Group Soul
- Group Monadic

Although these higher bodies are more refined and exist on more expanded planes of manifestation compared to the physical, etheric, astral and mental planes, they are still expressing in the form levels. As you will see in the next chapter, the activation of these higher bodies works hand in hand with the process of spiritual initiation.

After the activation of these higher bodies, the initiate expands into the experience of the solar planes, and then into the galactic, universal and cosmic levels.

It is worth nothing that there are lower and higher levels, or bandwidth of expression, within each of the planes and bodies.

The Physical- Etheric Body and the Physical Plane

Everything is energy, even science has caught up with this reality now. Even physical matter is, when you look at it closely enough, but charged particles of energy vibrating at different rates and in different ways, and interacting accordingly. The etheric body of living things is like a finer energetic template of the solid-liquid-gas bit of a body. It includes various levels of ethers, including heat, electricity, magnetic energy and light. It is still a physical form, but not one solid enough for most people's physical eyesight to see. When someone stands close to you, however, you may not see them, but you may feel a tangible presence, even if they are not touching you. If you put your hands close together but not touching, you may feel an energy there, something tangible rather than empty space. The etheric body includes a complex fine web of energy channels and centres, and is what hands-on healers and other therapists, like acupuncturists, usually worked on by addressing physical energetics rather than strictly physical matter. It is the level where chi, or life force flows. Electricity, magnetism and light are held within the physical structure through the etheric body. The level and vibration of these physical energies conditions our level of physical health. Everything we consume, do and engage with can alter our etheric vibration, from the energy in the food we eat, to the environment we spend a lot of time in, to our own through-patterns, emotions and attitudes. If the energy of our etheric body is not doing well, then it is only a matter of time until it eventually manifests as poor health outcomes. This is why sunlight or nature can have such a healing effect on our physical health: it is an energetic rather than purely physical interaction. Being bathed in good, higher-vibrational and harmonious energy re-attunes our own etheric energy, which in turns ripples its effects into the physical. Some radiant energy, like sunlight, can absorb into the solid-liquid-gas bits of the body in order to restore health and balance.

Remember that everything is energy, including the solid parts; they simply vibrate at a lower rate than the invisible form levels. We are energy through and through, including on the physical level. This accounts for the body-mind connection, whereby our beliefs, thoughts, attitudes and emotions can have a very direct impact on our physical health (and vice versa). We are interconnected energetic beings, straddling a few different planes of experience. All levels of our being are interconnected, just as we are energetically interconnected with our environment. Sadly, the way we live our modern lives, distant from nature, out of synch with our daily cycles of light and dark, isolated from our communities, and eating unnatural ultra-processed food, is contributing bad energy to our physical, emotional and mental health.

The Emotional body and the Astral Plan

Just like the physical body, the astral body and the mental body have a higher and lower bandwidth of experience and expression. The lower emotional level is where we experience our most primal, animalistic and negative emotions: instinctual emotions such as survival fear, territoriality, fear and terror, anger, jealousy, spite, hatred, anxiety, shame, depression and self-preservation. Emotions experienced on the lower astral plane are either about the animal nature or about fear, which the soul experiences as contracting and causing separation. In the middle levels of the emotional plane are conditional transactional love, sentiment, emotional control and emotional glamour.

Glamour results from lying to ourselves on the emotional level. It is the misty emotional version of the illusions we experience on the mental plane when we bullshit ourselves with falsehoods. Glamour usually acts as an energetic drug on our emotions, making us feel "good" but in a unhealthy way. It provides the appearance of comforting emotional blankets and instant relief from inconvenient emotions we otherwise would experience but is actually a form of manipulation of our own emotions, usually to avoid uncomfortable ones. We can glamour ourselves, but we can also use our own emotional energy to also glamour others as we wrap them up in the glamour we produce. This is like a spell, and is why the terms 'To glamour' someone exists. It is actually a form of dark magic, because it is about using our energy to manipulate experience and outcomes in a way which serves the selfish, fearful, egoic self.

This middle level of the emotional body is less instinctive and survival-oriented, but still focused within a sense of separateness, self-orientation and conditionality. It is however more functional and socialised than the lower shadowy emotions. The higher emotional body is where we experience more refined emotions: hope, emotional gratitude, emotional love, emotional joy or contentment, emotional peace, generosity or equanimity. These emotions are of a higher vibration, uplifting to the embodied soul's experience. Higher emotions make us feel more connected, selfless, open, and more willing to love and be loved without conditions. While lower emotions engender contraction of our energy, away from Soul and away from love, higher emotions expand our energy so we feel part of something larger than ourselves. A surge of higher emotions usually accompany peak spiritual experiences. This eruption of higher vibrational energy into the system then can have a detoxing effect on the emotional body, causing a catharsis of unresolved emotions. These higher emotions are the closest emotional expression of the higher dimensional experiences and qualities that an advanced soul holds and feels. Spiritual Masters seek to ground, embody and radiate the higher love they experience and embody into the world. This is one of the most important goals of achieving God Realisation: to give back in service. Enlightenment is not about selfishly blissing out on some higher plane, but about becoming a channel through which spiritual love, light, wisdom and truth can be brought into the world to help the evolution of Gaia. Finding ways to appropriately express and ground higher love vibrations through the lower bodies is part of how advanced souls can serve and bring more love into the world. Higher emotions are how these higher qualities, which vibrate in the bandwidth of unconditional love and above, can be expressed on the emotional level. The Master uses all of their lower bodies in the same way: the physical-etheric body can exudes peace, comfort, strength, and be the loving touch which nurtures another. The mind can also be used to radiate higher refined mental vibrations like illumination, compassionate understanding and spiritualised intelligence. It is of note that the astral plane is a real mishmash of energy, as it encompasses anything from dark selfish emotions to warmer ones, currents of glamours and astral constructs of people's secret little fantasy lives. The astral plane, as a plane of existence, is also where the dark lodge–the organised body of dark initiates on this planet–centres its activities. The White Lodge–the body of initiates on the path of love and light–centres its activities on the various levels of the mental plane, depending on the level of the initiates in question.

The Mental Body and the Mental Plane

The mental plane comprises its own set of sublevels. Before we explore them, I wish to debunk a common fallacy: the brain is not your mind! The brain is a physical organ, which acts as a switchboard allowing the interface between the mental body an the physical body. Sensory and experiential input from the physical level is translated by the nervous system into signals, which pass through the brain and alert the various bodies of what is happening. The signals are conveyed to the mental body, when then responds according to what it knows and the processes it is able to carry out. The response of the mental body is then carried back to the physical body in order to generate movement, words or any kind of chosen response. The screen of one's mind is clearly a vast and complex realm, within which visual memories can unfold, voices can be heard, hopes and plans can be visualised. To believe that all of this could happen inside a physical organ is nonsensical. The mental body is the body of mental matter through which we experience on the mental plane.

The lower mind includes the instinctive mind, the habit mind and the conscious mind (aka the monkey mind). The instinctive mind is where our animalistic and primal mental processes occur, or in other words the reptilian brain, or hindbrain-related functions. The habitual mind stores subconscious and procedural information. This is the mental knowledge about things and tasks that you no longer think about. This may include driving, brushing your teeth or the way to you best friend's house. Once upon a time, you had to think consciously about these things when you first learnt them. Once these task or information became familiar and habitual, it became subconscious and stored in the habit mind levels. Information can usually be retrieved at will from the habit mind, if one focuses on remember consciously. The next sublevel, the conscious mind, is the one most people are overly familiar with. This is the 'thinker' and is actually the top level of the lower mind. This is where we think, deduct, plan, strategise, create and store beliefs, perspectives, form opinions, talk to ourselves and consciously rehearse information (often with a view to store it into the habit mind). Sadly, most people over-identify with this level of their being; they think that the little voice and self-concept created in their mind is who they are. This is a limitation of course, because the beliefs we create about who we think we are, which we store in our lower mind, are not the truth of who we are. This personality self-concept is only a structure, like a role that we create in order to function and interact in the world. This personality idea is not always an authentic representation of our true self, and is always a limitation imposed on our own potential to be so much more.

The mind is a wonderful tool, but a terrible master. The lower mind is basically a mix between a library and an informational calculator. Memory processes store information we learn into the various levels of the lower mind (instinct, habits and conscious mind). Then, the mind uses the information it has stored in order to work out how to solve problems, how to find solutions to fulfil one's needs. Using the conscious mind is a constant process of questioning and answering ourselves. "How do I get to work?".... Monkey-mind computer searches the information you have stored in your memory banks and pulls out relevant results as it sees it.... The answer: "Based on previously stored or learnt information, this is how you can get to work". In a way, it is not too different from an internet search engine: you input a request, and based on what you ask, how you ask it and the information which is stored on the web, it puts together an answer. Just like a search engine, the answers can vary wildly based on the complexity and clarity of the question asked, and the quality of the information already entered. Just like a search engine, the lower mind can be very useful for concrete tasks and practical planning, and problem solving. The lower mind is very good at making connections between already available bits of data. It is therefore also very good at combining previously learnt information into new shapes to create different solutions or expressions with what you already know and have already stored in your mind library. This is also how beliefs and opinions are created and then stored in the mind: information is gathered, connected into a coherent narrative or belief, and then stored as some sort of truth. But it is not truth; it is simply a subjective interpretation of facts, which is then frozen in time and stored as a false eternal absolute. Beliefs, like everything stored in the mind, can only contain the past because the past is all the conscious mind knows. What the lower mind is useless for is coming up with completely new knowing, or answering questions which require information that is not already stored into its monkey-mind library. Like a search engine that lacks the information necessary to answer your question properly, the conscious mind will attempt to give you the best answer it can, but it will be at best an approximation, and at worse completely erroneous. The conscious mind is clever at connecting and combining existing and subjectively interpreted information. This can appear to be creative, because original combinations of existing information can easily pass for 'new' information. The reality is that combining existing elements in a different order is not the same as coming up with something truly novel. The lower mind is, therefore, unable to come up with truly, completely new ideas. All the lower mind knows is what you have already experienced and learnt until now. That's all it's got to work with! If you try to ask the lower mind questions about things you don't know yet, have not experienced , and which you cannot simply work out by computing existing stored information, then the conscious mind becomes useless. It's like asking someone who has never left their hometown what it's like to travel the world extensively. It can't really tell you! The best their lower mind can do is draw from stuff they've seen on TV or read online, and then combine these unit of theoretical data to make shit up! It is all second-hand information filtered through the lenses of someone who's never had the actual experience. All you are going to get is a very limited, imagined, probably distorted understanding. I once studied with a girl who had lived in hot places her entire life, and never experienced snow. As part of a class exercise one day, she was asked to describe the experience of being outside in the snow. Having never experienced it herself, she had created a set of beliefs about what snow would be like based on movies, her experience of rain and Christmas-treat flavours. She imagined snow making noticeable noise as it hit your face or the ground, and tasting like mint! This just goes to show that we can create any belief we choose, but this does not make them the truth.

This is why the conscious mind is a wonderful tool, but a very poor Master. The conscious mind is your servant, to use for the management of daily living tasks, storing useful information and problem solving. But it should never be what guides your life decisions, nor should you consult it when you seek higher truth. Thankfully, there are other levels of mind which can assist you with that.

The lower bodies include the physical, astral and lower mental body, which is up to the conscious mind level. The lower bodies are termed "lower" because they exist, in vibrational terms, below the level of the individual soul vehicle. The individual soul vessel resides smack in the middle of the mental plane, on what is called the Buddhic plane. Remember that the soul vehicle itself is still a form vehicle, spawned to house a spark of the spiritual essence of the soul tree of which you are. The soul bridges between the spiritual energy of the higher planes and the lower form levels, facilitating our ability to incarnate. Beyond housing a stream of the Soul Tree's energy, the Soul is also the repository for the accumulated life experience integrated over many form incarnations of that Soul. This includes completed learning stored as wisdom, unfinished learning, unresolved pain, and conflicted energy. All of this stored experience results from the choices that the soul extensions, the leaves of that Soul, have made over their many lives through time and space. This accumulated store of experience, wisdom and unresolved issues is the karma that this soul bears. I will explore the notion of karma into more details in chapter 4. The Soul vehicle exists on the mental plane, above the levels of lower mind, but beneath the higher mental sub-planes.

If the lower mind has its limits beyond the realm of practical application, and the soul is a bridge storing experience from its many soul extension incarnations, what are we supposed to do in order to truly access new ideas and inspiration? Or to find answer to our existential questions? The answer: look higher!

There are two levels of accessing information from levels higher than our little monkey mind. The first is Soul. Once we become spiritually awake and activated to Soul identification level, we can begin to draw on the accumulated wisdom the Soul has accumulated from its many lifetimes journey through time. As we will see in our next chapter, when you have successfully undergone the required initiations, you can become fully informed by the energy of the Soul that you are a leaf on. This means you can draw on the wisdom and learning from experiences that you, as a Soul but not as a human person, have had in other leaf-lives. This is nothing that you as a person have experienced, and your lower mind does not know it, but the Soul knows it and has experienced it. Only by evolving to a certain level can be begin to access the knowing from other soul extensions of the same Soul that we are a leaf on. The second way to access truly new information, higher truth or answers to larger existential questions is to access the levels of higher mind, and beyond.

The higher mind is still part of the mental plane, but above the Buddhic level, and therefore above where Soul resides. Here we gradually expand into the realms of ideas, concepts and eventually, at its highest level, into the level of pure Knowing. The higher mind is where our individual soul vehicle can connect in incremental steps to something greater than itself. It is where the Soul can interact with, and overlap a little into the Mind of God. Contrarily to the levels beneath it, the higher mental plane is a level which is free of the fear, illusion and glamour. It is also a level whereby the individual can connect with the collective as the higher mental planes transcend the personal individual mind and offer a realm of shared mind. The realm of ideas and concepts is one where we each have a personal channel into, yet also one which is shared with the rest of humanity and beyond. Only those with a degree of monastic and spiritual development can access the higher mental planes, which some refer to as levels of divine inspiration, or the levels of their muse. Truly inspired artists, scientists, philosophers and innovators may receive ideas and conceptual downloads from the higher mental planes. This is why several people can appear to have had the same ideas at the same time; they simply all picked up on the same broadcast! New ideas can spread like ripples in a pond, especially when they are focused upon, given energy to and built upon. Genuine inspiration is when the idea comes to a person from the higher mental planes, if they are receptive and an appropriate channel to ground that inspiration into the world. This differs from simple human cleverness, which constructs and reorder from bits of previously held knowledge. Both can be useful, but only genuine inspiration will have the magic touch to be transformative, inspirational and healing.

The level of concepts and conceptual understanding is more expanded and abstract than the realm of ideas. Indeed, the higher the plane, the more abstract its reality. The level of concepts can be tapped into, communicated and grounded into reality, just as the level of ideas can. Two people who share the same reality and the same level of higher mental access will have a much easier time communicating with each other, mind to mind. Communication of higher reality with people who cannot access those higher mental reality is more difficult and requires translation. To make such concepts more accessible and useful to everyone, we can receive from the expanded-ness of a concept, and then derive the more concrete forms of ideas. These ideas can then be translated into more concrete thought forms, and then articulated into words, objects, images, or procedures. The process of working with the higher mind is one of accessing a greater, more expansive level of Knowing beyond our own individual little minds, and then filtering down and translating it into the lower levels of forms. This is how Divine Knowing and new ideas can be used to create something novel, make available new information, set in motion inspired actions and make the world a better place.

The final level of the higher mind is the level of pure Knowing. This level is only accessible to Souls who have, through extensive personal and spiritual development over lifetimes, developed the ability to connect to information stored in the Mind of God. One may say that the process of spiritual initiation is one of gradual expansion into the Mind of God. Contrarily to common misconception, a relative minority of people have activated enough to work effectively with the various levels of the higher mind. The level of ideas is accessed by more people than the level of concepts; and the level of pure Knowing is accessed by a relative few.

Many people confuse the clever conscious-mind skill of recombining bits of existing knowledge with that of accessing genuine creativeness, but they are not the same. When one's mind is developed and expanded enough to reach into those levels, they can access, download, channel and simply 'Know' new information which comes from the accumulated eternal experience of their Soul Tree, Soul Forest and the Mind of God. This experience of pure Knowing is profound and requires no logical explanation or proof of the lower five senses. The experience is one of one's mind becoming one with a particular Knowing within the mind of God. In that moment of communion, the information received from the levels of pure Knowing is simply known as absolutely true. It simply and irrevocably just is. It is not something that egos existing in the illusion of separateness are likely to understand. Attempting to explain it to someone who has never experienced it, or trying to prove that the information retrieved from such a level is true, is often difficult or impossible. One either knows, or does not know, and that is all there is to it. Your capacity to translate and ground higher Knowing is, however, contingent on your level of energetic and psychological clarity. If your human vehicle is full of fear, rigid beliefs and egoic distortions, any information or knowing that comes through will be coloured and tainted by your fear and distortions. Even the clearest water, when channelled through a dirty pipe, will come out muddy. The process of emotional and psychological purification is therefore absolutely key in spiritual work. Being able to access the higher planes is one thing; being able to translate and ground what we learn with clarity is another. Concurrently, not even higher Truth, perceived in a moment of spiritual clarity and inspiration, should ever be forced onto others. A revelation may have been just for you, or meant to inform your work. If it is meant to be relayed to others as teaching or guidance, then it must be offered, but not imposed. Everyone has the free will to decide their own reality, for better or for worse. All we can hope is that their hearts and mind are open enough to feel the recognition and resonance with the Truth essence of what you share. If it feels true to their hearts, then the Knowing itself has conveyed itself to them. It is not about you, in the end. You are simply the messenger.

Above and Beyond….

Are there other levels beyond the higher mind? Yes. There are higher bodies which can be activated, each of them granting the ability to experience and interact on a new plane of Creation. Here is a very brief review of some of these bodies and the planes they exist upon. (*For more detailed information, please check Michael King's YouTube video The Science of Ascension, on the Cosmosis® Mentoring Centre YouTube channel. See Chapter 7 for details*).

The Atmic body is the next body above the Buddhic vehicle and is considered the first of the light-bodies. It exists on the Atmic plane, which is the level whereby the individual soul gains beginner insights into aspects of Divine will and aspects of the Divine Plan.

Next comes the Monadic body, which exists on the Monadic Plane. This level allows access to a higher expression of Divine Intelligence and to access the wisdom of the Oversoul

After this comes the Logoic body, which exists on the Logoic plane. This is the level of beginning to experience Divine Grace and oneness with the Life itself, in service of with Divine Will and Divine Love, and access to the Knowing and wisdom of the Monad. This is way beyond the levels of anything personal or individual.

Beyond the Logoic level are the Group Soul body and the Group Monadic body, which include the experience of co-creatorship, and then beyond into Solar levels and more, where we tap into the experience of Creatorship. But we are now way past what is relevant to almost everyone on this planet at present. To expand further would risk only indulging the egoic mind as it tries to grasp something it cannot possibly grasp. What really matters for the reader is how to wake up from being a little leaf, amnesic to its true spiritual nature and blown in the winds of life, to re-membering ourselves as part of a larger Soul Tree. The process of spiritual awakening and growth is one of remembering and realising our already existing spiritual nature, as a small part of a much larger being. Once we begin to remember, we must then do the work on grounding our new knowing, and walking the talk of new states of being in our daily life.

Dimensions

The notions of plane and dimension are often used interchangeably, yet are two interrelated but different things. Planes are the levels of the form, or manifest, aspect of Creation, while dimensions are the being, or un-manifest, aspect. Planes are vibrational levels of the structure of Creation. Dimensions are the quality of reality we experience within the planes.

If we liken planes to the floors in an apartment block, dimensions would be the interior ambience, decor, spaciousness and view from these different floors. The lowest level apartments may be smaller, cramped, with no windows. This will condition our experience within it. The higher level may be wide, bright, with a seemingly endless view and full of good gadgets. Although all inhabitant of the building live within the same building, those on the higher floor would have a drastically different experience and worldview than those living on the lower floors. A plane is the framework, or vibrational structure of a certain level of manifest creation; dimension is the state of consciousness and state of being we experience when we are aware on that plane.

Each plane of Creation therefore goes hand in hand with a particular dimensional experience. The lower the plane and dimension, the lower its vibration and the lesser its degree of expansiveness. The higher the plane and dimension experienced, the higher the vibration of the experience and the more expansive it is. As a creature polarises their consciousness and sense of identification on a plane of existence, they will experience the dimensional experience which goes with that plane. The vast majority of human beings experience life in the third-dimension although we are by nature multidimensional beings, given that we have physical, emotional and mental bodies. Even spiritual unawakened human beings therefore encompass within their experience the first dimension associated with our genetic material and water, the second dimension associated with our primitive hindbrain and body elementals, and the third dimension of the individual personality experience. But humans are not usually aware of the first and second dimension. The third-dimensional consciousness overrides the others because it contains the other two, and it is where most humans identify and focus their consciousness. This is how it works: any creature whose experience expands across more than one plane of existence will polarise their consciousness in the highest dimension of their experience. This is unless they allow themselves to get triggered into a lower level of identification, and drop their consciousness to a lower level. Sadly, this is the effect that alcohol, certain strong negative primal emotions or certain drugs can have on a person: they can trigger some degree of regression into animal behaviour and the instinctive linear focus associated with the second dimension.

Here is a quick run-through of the dimensional consciousness associated with each of the planes that are currently achievable for spiritual disciples while incarnate in a human body.

- The physical plane is qualified by first dimensional consciousness, which is one-point consciousness. The experience of the first dimension is isolation. It is completely self-focused and immediate. It is just me, right here, right now, and nothing else. There is no awareness of anything outside of self, yet one can explore whole universes of reality within the self. This is the dimension experienced by the mineral kingdom, water, devas and elementals, individual molecules, atoms and the genetic codes of creatures. This dimensional awareness of this level of ourselves is unconscious for human beings.

- Second-dimensional consciousness is the one-directional linear consciousness of distance. Where first dimensional consciousness was awareness of point, the second dimension is also the awareness of a vector direction, or the line between two points. The focus is between me and an external object, right here, right now, and is very... two-dimensional! Attention is limited to me, the avoidance of threats, the obtaining of the object of my desires or needs, and what I can use to get them. While we now have a sense of something outside of self, there is no real sense of passing time, no self-awareness, and there is no reflection or planning. It is simply me and the object of my attention connected by a line of attention or action in this moment. There is an immediacy to this dimension as everything is happening now, and is conditioned by instinct, urges, programs, desires and needs: "I want this thing outside of me, and so I am propelled into doing what is necessary to get what I need or want". This is the dimensional consciousness of the plant kingdom and the lower levels of the animal kingdom, which are driven by the collective consciousness of their species and the need to survive, feed and procreate. This is a very "tribal" state, guided by species-specific identity, feeling completely a part of nature, and driven by the primal instinct. For human beings, this dimension of consciousness is centred in the primitive brain functions, the hindbrain, which governs our biological functions, the urge to procreate and our autonomic nervous system. This dimensional level of the human experience is unconscious for most people, but through deep self-awareness practice and meditation, we can become more aware of this dimension of our existence and gain some control over it. This is how Masters, or yogis are able to affect some of their biological functions, such as slowing down their heart rate or breathing to an impressive extent, or control their body-temperature. For a human, becoming more aware on this dimension can fill us with an awe and deep respect for the complexity and perfection of life.

- Third-dimensional consciousness is awareness of the point, the line and volume, and is qualified by the experience of contraction. In the previous dimensions, creatures are guided by the group soul-or group mind-of their particular species. The third dimension relies on individuation, which means the creature is guided by their own individual soul and individual mind. This is the dimensional consciousness that most evolved animal and the vast majority of human beings live within. When animals evolve and become almost ready to move into the human kingdom, they begin to individuate, and develop the seed of having their own individual mind and soul, independently from the collective mind of their species. This is what qualifies the human kingdom as different from the animal kingdom: we exist as separate individuals, in a way that animals are not.

This dimension still features a sense of struggle to survive, to procreate, to be safe and to feel good, but it introduces a greater capacity for thought and feelings. This dimension features the concept of time, of cause and effect, the ability to connect and relate multiple objects in relation to us and each other, the ability to reflect on the past and plan the future, and the ability to choose more than one perspective. This is how human souls are able to learn: by tracking cause and consequence and by reflecting and planning. In order for this tracking to be possible, everything has to be slow and discernible so we can trace and connect the effects of our choices and actions. This slowing down makes this dimension clunky, hard work, and holding much inertia. While the third dimensions brings a more complex awareness of the world around us, there is still a sense of being separate from it and therefore limited. This creates a sense of separation from the environment and from other people, and can even generate a feeling of 'me against the world'. In order to satisfy our wants and needs, or achieve our goals, we must force our little will onto the surrounding objects and people. This is the realm of the human ego, the conscious realm. There is no sense of interconnectedness with the collective, nor remembrance of past lives. Human beings polarised in third dimensional reality do not sense higher dimensions and may not even believe that such spiritual realms exist.

When the human creature begins to realise that they create their own reality, they are almost ready to move into the fourth dimension. Self-reflection, the development of deep inner self-awareness and a more loving character, meditation, creative work and dream work can support us to expand from the third-dimension into the fourth.

Fourth dimensional consciousness includes the awareness of point, line, volume and time in the experience of the Soul. The quality of fourth dimensional consciousness is flow and is the consciousness of the astral, mental, Buddhic and Atmic bodies. This is also the dimension where non-physical beings, spirit guides, and archetypes exist, bridging the physical and non-physical realms in order to serve the process of evolution and enlightenment. As before, this dimension incorporates the previous dimensions within itself, like Russian dolls stacked dolls around each other.

Fourth-dimensional consciousness still carries a sense of linear time and complex perspective-taking as in the third dimension, but instead of experiencing everything our environment as separate from one another and separate from me, we begin to feel and know the interconnectedness of all things. We still experience ourselves as an individual, but feel how we are connected to our environment and through time. We know and sense the flow of cause and consequence as two-sides of the same coin. Interactions between all things become more apparent and I become more conscious of my input in causing things to happen. This dimension is less clunky and more flowing than the previous dimension. Manifesting through our thoughts and feelings is a much faster process in the fourth dimension than it was in the third, and we can change and shift much faster in this dimension. At this level, we become increasingly aware that it is our thoughts and feelings which create and filter our reality, and the effects are felt much quicker in our own experience.

The fourth dimension is also where time expands to include the Soul's timeline, where a feeling memory of all the other third-dimensional embodiments of our Soul and Soul Group are perceived. The fourth dimension includes intense experiences of unconditional love, spiritualised passion, spiritual creativity and requires the profound integration of spirituality into our daily lives. Be aware, however, that the fourth dimension still features the presence of both light and dark, love and fear. Being active in the fourth dimension is a big responsibility because darkness and evil can quickly be manifested by fourth-dimensional Souls who choose to indulge fear.

Some evolved Souls are born already holding a connection to fourth-dimensional consciousness. These Souls must work hard to fully ground their presence and consciousness into the concrete third-dimension of Earth life, although it can feel hostile to their more refined senses and remembered higher reality. If they do not ground properly, they risk going through life ungrounded and out-of-touch, which can cause challenges in manifesting earthly success, but also give them an airy-fairy quality and naivety which makes them easy targets for less scrupulous Souls.

- Fifth dimensional consciousness is associated with actualisation on the Monadic plane and activating the Monadic body. It is qualified by the experience of Oneness. It includes the perception of point, line, volume, time and in-dwelling Soul life. Again, this dimension of consciousness includes all previous dimensions: we maintain our sense of individual self, but it is contained within the tangibly felt sense and knowing of the Oneness of All Life and All things. This is more than an intellectual or philosophical concept; it is a fully felt and experienced reality. It is unity-consciousness. The initiate feels the presence of God-Goddess within All things, and knows themselves to be a small part of All That Is.

In this dimension, the experience of time and space becomes less linear, and the Soul experiences less of the limitations of previous dimensions. The fifth-dimensional self exists in the time experience of the Eternal Now. On this Monadic plane, our feelings manifest instant outcomes.

At this level, there is only love, which facilitates our connection with our Higher Self. Fear cannot exist in this dimension. If we engage in fear while holding fifth-dimensional consciousness, then our consciousness will automatically drop back to the fourth dimension. Fourth-dimensional consciousness puts us in a state called isolated unity: a pervasive and expansive sense of unconditional love and acceptance of all things, and All Life, which we fully know and feel to be an extension of the One Life that we are a unified part of too.

This is the beginning of hosting an ascended consciousness. Beings who exist on this plane can easily change form, and move fast through both time and space simply by willing and desiring it. Movement on this level feels like a mix of flying and swimming. At the same time, the fifth-dimensional self is still aware of our third and fourth-dimensional selves, which are contained within our higher experience. The physical body still moves at a third-dimensional pace, regardless of the pace we can move at on higher levels! There is a clear and unified multi-dimensional experience on this level; we are aware of the lower and higher levels of self, below and above the fifth dimension, and feeling a unity between them all.

- Sixth dimensional consciousness comes with actualisation on the Logoic plane and the Logoic body. It incorporates the awareness of point, line, volume, time, Soul life, and the life of the indwelling Spirit. The quality of experience on this level is Is-ness. The state of being held on this level is All That Is.

Building on the previous dimension's experience of Oneness, we now expand into the complete transcending of judgment and duality, as we realise that everything simply is. There is no good or bad, no right or wrong, no opinion, but a general relativeness which allows everything to simply be what it is. Guided by this level, we can still be discerning and make choices accordingly, but we no longer judge or perceive life through the lens of duality or separateness of any kind. Everything becomes relative, ever-changing and a non-issue, like an intricate, purposeful tapestry. This is the dimension of grace and equanimity.

This dimension is the beginning of Divine Illumination and Divine Awareness. To achieve this level, we must be completely in heart consciousness, surrender, acceptance, allowance, purity, clarity and openness.

Only the most advanced Master Souls of our planet, and their inner plane ashrams, exist on this level. At this point, it becomes difficult to express into language the experience of these higher dimensions.

- The Seventh dimension is the experience of the Group Soul levels. It incorporates the awareness of point, line, volume, time, Soul life, the indwelling Spirit and Source presence as Systemic Verity. This level is qualified by the experience of Pure Awareness. At this level, we still experience Is-ness, but also begin to experience oneness with Source: the awakening of Source awareness. We also hold a state of being called Co-Creator, with is an all-encompassing essential Unity, and the full-blown reality of the Group Soul level of the larger being we are a part of.

- The eight dimension includes the awareness of point, line, volume, time, Soul life, the indwelling Spirit, Source Presence as Systemic Verity, and Source

Presence as Systemic Deity. This is reality at the level of the Group Monadic body, and with it comes a state of being called Essential Unity.

- Ninth dimensional consciousness includes the awareness of point, line, volume, time, Soul life, the indwelling Spirit, Source Presence as Systemic Verity, Source Presence as Systemic Deity and the Existential Trinity. This is the dimensional level of the Great White Lodge of Sirius and is impossible to describe.

- The Tenth dimension incorporates the awareness of point, line, volume, time, Soul life, the indwelling Spirit, Source Presence as Systemic Verity, Source Presence as Systemic Deity, the Existential Trinity and the Non-Existential Trinity. This is the reality of the Solar Lord who en-souls our solar system, Helios-Vesta.

- The eleventh dimensions includes the awareness of point, line, volume, time, Soul life, the indwelling Spirit, Source Presence as Systemic Verity, Source Presence as Systemic Deity, the Existential Trinity, the Non-Existential Trinity and the Unified Cosmic Field. This is the reality of the Personality aspect who en-souls our galaxy, Lord Melchior.

- The twelfth dimension is the beginning of the Universal levels of experience. These are the levels of the dimensional reality of the en-souling Personality aspect of our Universe, Lord Melchizedek.

- Beyond this—on planes 25 to 48—are the Cosmic levels. And it does not stop there!

As you can see, the reality that most people experience on this planet is but the bare beginnings of what is possible for us as evolving aspects of Source.

****

Achieving and holding those higher dimensional states go hand-in-hand with the process of spiritual initiation, and the awakening and activation of higher aspects of self. We explore the process of spiritual initiation in our next chapter.

Before we do, I wish to offer important clarity and humility on the topic of achieving higher levels of consciousness. As a soul spiritually grows and evolves, it awakens to the reality that it is part of something greater. Slowly, gradually, we merge with and experiences ourselves to be a larger and larger part of that greater 'self', our Soul Tree. The leaf awakening to its true nature realises that it is part of the twig. As it grows it realises it is part of a branch, and then it realises that it is part of an even bigger branch. This continues until the individual soul knows itself to be both the individual leaf on planet earth, while simultaneously knowing itself to be the whole tree, and then the forest, and beyond! Therefore, each time a soul pushes into the next level of awakening and activation, its consciousness and sense of who and what we are involves a greater and greater chunk of its soul tree. With each step up this evolutionary initiation ladder, the consciousness of the soul expands into the next dimension of consciousness, the next level of reality. Although the evolving soul's sense of self and identification evolves as we undergo the process of spiritual activation and realisation, we still experience all levels, planes and dimensions of themselves right down to the physical and lower dimensional levels. The foundational human third-dimensional experience does not disappear, but becomes simply contained within and expanded upon by the more expansive dimensional reality of higher planes.

It is important to realise that it is the Soul who undergoes this transformation and expansion. If we use the metaphor of the human vehicle being a car, the Soul would be the driver. The Soul is changing, morphing and evolving into a more God-actualised expression, while the human vehicle remains a vehicle for the expression of what the Soul is becoming. The Soul is the one slowly becoming a Master Soul, not the human creature. It is the Soul whose reality and dimensional experience expand, while the human being is simply along for the ride, existing in its third-dimensional reality, yet encased and held in the Soul's reality. As we evolve and identify more fully as the Soul that we are, we eventually meet the criteria to affect the ascending-descension of Soul into the human body. Soul can ground its experience into form, but in this the human self is only a point of focus and a channel for the Soul's energy to express into the earth planes. The higher dimensions that Soul expands into can be felt by the human being, but it is not the human doing it.

This is where many spiritual seekers and disciples go wrong: they make it about their human ego. Their personality-self thinks that because they can connect higher levels of divinity, it makes them a demi-God, or that because they channel a higher being, then they must be this higher being! Making the experience of Spirit and Soul about the human egoic personality is foolish and destructive. It can, in the long term, only lead to a fall and loss of those higher realities. The human is a vessel for the Soul to experience and evolve, but this vessel can ever only be this: a vessel existing on the three lower planes, which the Soul, informs, directs and focuses through.

The job of the human self in this evolutionary equation is to become a more refined human, a clear channel, and a good servant to the Soul in charge. Mostly, this means clearing out the fear, separation and dysfunctional patterns which stand in the way of the in-dwelling Soul taking control of the human vehicle to undertake its process of transformation and enlightenment. It means loving ourselves, yet becoming truly selfless in surrendering to our Soul and Soul Tree's evolutionary destiny. Only by purifying the body, emotions and psyche of the human vehicle can we make it safe host for the Soul to anchor and take up residence here full time. The Soul must then continue its evolution, but also ground what it integrates in order to share it with the world, in service to All That Is. A clear and purified human vehicle can then be used as a resonator, through which the love, light and Knowing of the Higher Self can be grounded and expressed into the world. Everything we learn must be offered in service. This is the way. The process which facilitates this journey of expansion and realisation is spiritual initiation.

CHAPTER 3

Initiation

~ ~ ~

For some, the term initiation may evoke secret rituals conducted by mysterious robed figures. For others, it may evoke the ceremony of baptism, bat mitzvah, or perhaps the hazing rituals that mark one's entry into a prestigious school or fraternity. What all these examples have in common is the attempt, sometimes expressed poorly, to mark the transition out of a phase of one's life and into the beginning of a new one. The initiation rite marks a progression, an accession to something that was previously denied, but is now offered to those who qualify for it. Boiled down to its simplest elements, this is indeed what an initiation is.

Spiritual initiations define and mark the major milestones in levels of learning, activation and mastery along the path to Spiritual Ascension and God Realisation. Spiritual Ascension is the process of continuous awakening, spiritual purification and expansion which allows us to raise both our consciousness and our vibration, and regain access to higher levels of reality, greater levels of spiritual Knowing and the actualisation of our Spiritual potential, in, of and for Love. God Realisation is simply the process of realising what exists within the Mind of God, and realising the presence and potential of God within us. We must bring all that we know to become in alignment with and in service of what God knows. What is stored in the Mind of God is everything that has been experienced and learnt, and all the wisdom, truth and Knowing of every part of Creation, across the board, through all time until now. It is obvious that the Mind of God would know better than our little monkey brain! The little leaf on the Soul Tree must awaken to the truth, in increasing degrees, that it is part of God and one with God. To achieve God realisation, we must remove the veils of false being, illusion and separation within which we have entombed ours consciousness. We must remember our ultimate Divine nature, and become more like God by displaying amazing qualities of heart consciousness, enlightenment, spiritual intelligence, wisdom, Grace and selfless service to the Divine Plan. All that we can become already exists within the Mind of God; we only have to realise it, surrender to it and actualise it. The more we become in the image of God again (As above, so below!), the closer to Godhood will our state of being become, and the closer to Source we will return. Like attracts like.

In order to undergo spiritual initiation, we must earn our way into each stage of the process. One does not become one with higher levels of the Soul Tree without actualising energy and qualities which vibrate in sympathy with the true nature of the Higher Self. This is basic physics. Everything is energy vibrating at particular frequencies. Vibration was, after all, the original sound and light of God, The Word that was spoken, the light that suddenly was. Vibration made and set Creation in motion. In the world of vibration, like attracts like and energy will always seek to vibrate in harmony with what it is a part of. We recognise this dynamic easily within music. There is a reason music scales exist. A music scale is a set of particular notes which sound good together and express a particular mood, or feeling. We may not know why, but our senses and our soul respond to music. We simply know if something sounds harmonious or discordant. Some things go well together, creating harmony; some things don't, and create chaos and discord. It is the way of things. Enough research has been done on plants, in-utero babies, and physically or mentally sick patients to know that our bodies and minds respond to the particular harmony created by certain types of music. Play Mozart or some beautifully healing music to plants, unborn babies or sick patients over time, and the markers of health, well-being and positive stimulation will be observed. Play discordant, chaotic, violent metal music, and the markers of health and well-being will degrade. Everything responds to the energy it interacts with. Everything is vibrationally in relationship with and affecting everything else. Some of you may feel affronted at my description of metal music being degrading to the natural harmony of our vibration, but it is a simple fact. Mind you, I went through a phase in my mid-to-late teens when I listened to some melodic metal music. I could never bring myself to like the more extreme hard metal, which I experienced even then as just screaming and noise. Those teen years of my life, unsurprisingly, bubbled with anger, sadness, and discontent. My use of metal music was me searching for a mirror of my internal angst. The music reflected to me my frustration and despair, and became part of me processing my emergent backlog of unresolved feelings. My internal discord was more easily accessed and processed when I immersed myself in vibrations of musical angst. But once I healed and transcended these angry, pained teenage aspects, I lost interest and reoriented towards other types of music. Some people may use such music to indulge or energise their anger; I used it as a cathartic support.

The point is: everything works in response to vibration. Like attracts like, vibration seeks that which vibrates in synch with itself, unless interfered with. If you are full of fear, you will attract more fear. If you are full of love, you will attract more love. This is the basic understanding behind the Law of Manifestation exposed in popular works of new age spirituality about manifestation. What you put out comes back at you.

It therefore becomes obvious that in order to become one with more of our Soul Tree, we must learn to vibrate more in harmony with the natural essence and vibration of this greater spiritual being, which we are a part of. Choosing not to is choosing to remain in separation consciousness, encasing ourselves in our own separate reality and sense of self, which is discordant to our true spiritual nature. As long as we cling to the things which are in discordance with the vibration of our innate spiritual essence and higher self, the more the door to spiritual growth will be closed to us. When we transform, refine and shape the human vehicle to be more in the image of our inner spark of God self -The God within - we vibrate more in sympathy with the energy of the Soul Tree. Because of this, the Soul Tree's energy can gradually descend and ground into the human vehicle in order to inform us and hold a presence on the Earth plane. This is a process of ascending descension. The human vibration is raised and purified, which allows an ascension of our energy and consciousness into higher expressions, planes, and dimensions of experience. Simultaneously, the Soul Tree's energy descends into the now more refined human vessel. It is a two-way process. Human and Soul Tree are constantly reaching towards each other to bridge between heaven and earth. As the lower part rises in vibrational terms, the higher part descends and grounds a presence where its love is most needed: the

Earth plane. This is important to grasp because many religions and spiritual traditions have for too long placed enormous emphasis on the ascending part. This has generated a distorted sense that spiritual initiation is about escaping out of our 'bad' humanity in order to run away towards some blissful heaven. This escapist form of spirituality has caused too many spiritual disciples to be at war with themselves, rejecting their human-ness rather than seeking to spiritualise it. It is crucial we approach spirituality in an integrated way: refining and spiritualising body, mind and spirit into an integrated whole, so that Spirit can ground its presence. Let's face it, the love and enlightenment that our Higher Self can bring is much needed down here, on planet Earth. So why seek escape rather than help bring this planet back to a state of love and enlightenment?

A Brief Overview of the Spiritual Initiation Process

Each spiritual initiation is like a gateway. In order to be allowed to pass through each initiation stage and into the next level of spiritual evolution, we must meet certain criteria and demonstrate certain levels of proficiency. This includes the refinement of our character, motives and intentions, the realignment of our behaviour towards enlightened ideals, the purification of our body, emotions, mind and soul, the raising of our vibration and the expansion of our consciousness. To raise our vibration means to make our energy be of a higher frequency of vibration. As we know, Source exploded, expanded and subdivided, and then created levels and planes of manifestation. The lower the frequency of vibration, the more dense and concrete its manifestation, until it reached the state of physical matter. Logically, in order to reverse the process and re-ascend towards our Source, we must once again raise our frequency.

We do this in three main ways:

- By purifying our system of dense energies of fear and contraction which keep us stuck in density;

- By choosing loving and uplifting behaviours, attitudes and states of being;

- By allowing the influence and ingress of higher spiritual energies which help raise our frequency.

Lower energies of fear, such as jealousy, anger, hatred, resentment, victim-consciousness, selfishness, greed, pride or shame all vibrate at a lower frequency than higher energies such as hope, gratitude, compassion, purity of heart, wisdom, joy and courage. Therefore, as we clear the fear-based lower frequency and embrace higher vibrational states of love, our vibration naturally will lift. If In addition, if you invite the influence of higher spiritual energies into your life, through meditation, prayer, invocation and communion, then you will raise your vibration further over time.

Each initiation involves the demonstration of self-mastery and the purification of our energy and character. This goes hand in hand with the achievement of higher light quotients. Light quotients are literally the percentage of enlightenment present within your soul, and then shining through the human vehicle. Why does enlightenment matter? Because spiritual light is produced when spirit descends and fuses into matter. This occurs as part of the ascending descension process: the spiritual aspirant raises their vibration towards that of Spirit, while Spirit descends to hold a presence within the human vehicle. The more Spirit resides within the vehicle, the more fusion and light is produced. This is simple spiritual physics.

Another aspect of the initiation process is the clearing of karma. More will be explored on this topic later, but clearing the energetic impacts that we set in motion through our choices and behaviours over time is a big part of what removes barriers to our progression through the initiations. It begins with clearing karma from this life, and learning to make better choices as a result, and then expands into clearing the karma from other incarnations and embodied aspects of the Soul Tree as we progress. Where we are at in this karmic clearing process defines our planetary karmic balance.

Ultimately, you must be the change you seek, by becoming a more faithful expression of your Soul Tree. Return to be in God's image. Be the fertile soil ready to receive the seeds of what you wish to grow into. This may mean faking it until you make it for a time. If you live as a Master would, and clear everything within you or in your life which opposes this while practicing masterful behaviour, then you will eventually become a master. The initiation sets the curriculum of the key aspects of becoming a more God-like expressions of our true eternal self, in gradual stages as described below.

Before we study the various levels of planetary initiations, I wish to clarify that the criteria and skills to be mastered for each initiation are not about complete and absolute perfection, especially in the early initiations. Nothing in the initiation process, nor in real life, is a purely linear process. Each initiation requires the demonstration of high levels of mastery and ability in the area pertaining to each initiation, but it does not have to be a perfect score right from the early initiations. Areas of mastery are revisited and further refined as the disciple grows into further initiations. The further the initiate progresses into the higher initiations, the higher the scores expected to complete each initiation successfully. The standards of mastery are refined and held to increasingly higher standards with each initiation. As the initiate undergoes the higher initiations, they will have to polish any areas from previous initiations where they may have scraped through with a minimum pass mark. Lessons repeat at higher turns of the spiral, demanding a much higher level of performance and mastery. The completion of planetary ascension requires a near perfect pass mark. To enter the higher ranks of the true God Realised Planetary Masters, we cannot get away with anything! The grade of mastery demonstrated at each initiation will directly facilitate the spiritualisation of the four-body system, impacting the levels of spiritual light present and produced, i.e. light quotients.

The pass marks and quotient achieved at each initiation can also vary from initiate to initiate. Like with university students, there are those who pass their exams with just the minimum mark required to pass, and others who excel and achieve a high score. Like school students, not all initiates of a given degree are equal in the depth and breadth of their mastery. Whatever area of weakness have been left unattended in previous initiations will always catch up with us in later stages of the process. If at all possible, I would recommend to go for more than minimum pass marks, because weak areas can easily cause problem in later initiations.

In addition, light and love quotients required at each stage of the planetary initiation process vary based on where human mass consciousness humanity is at. The more dark and primitive the state of evolution of the mass of humanity, the lower the scores and quotient required to pass each initiation. This is because the standards for spiritual initiates are set based on how far ahead of the collective of humanity they are, in evolutionary terms. As humanity, as a whole, evolves over time, and as more light grounds into the Earth plane, so the benchmarks for each initiation rise. This is evolution within evolution; everything expands, improves and refines not only within themselves but also relative to each other. The quotients I give you are relevant for now, but will eventually change in the future as our collective race evolves. Many thousands of years ago, the third initiation marked the completion of planetary ascension. Then, as humanity evolved, it became the fourth initiation. As human evolution and enlightenment gradually grew over the centuries, it became the fifth, then the sixth and then the seventh. Only recently has the ninth initiation become the completion point of planetary ascension. After completing planetary ascension, the initiate moves into the realm of Solar, Galactic, Universal and Cosmic ascension and initiation. 100% light quotient on the planetary level only represents 10% Cosmic light quotient. Everything is on this relative scale because as our consciousness reaches new realms and levels, everything is bigger and there is so much more to learn and master. When we reach the top of the food chain of planetary ascension, we are a big fish in a small pond; once we move beyond the planetary sphere of evolution, we become a small fish in a big pond.

Evolution before Initiation

Everything and everyone evolves. Evolution will happen whether we want it or not. It is not up to us, little self-obsessed human creatures, to decide the fate of an infinite Divine Creation. We are but tiny parts of the body of this Creation and shouldn't assume our free will isn't contained within a larger framework. We may have free will about whether we follow the memo gracefully or kicking and screaming, and about how and when we accept our part in the unfolding greater plan of evolution; but we don't have the free will to decide if evolution happens. I am afraid that vote has already been cast and this type of decision is way above our spiritual pay-grade. Our choice is therefore a question of whether we choose to fight against the process of evolution, or partner with it. Souls who resist the process of evolution or ignore it completely are not on the spiritual path. They are evolving, as every creature must, albeit slowly, but they are not consciously engaged in the process of spiritual evolution. Bear in mind that being consciously engaged with our evolution does not automatically infer being engaged in religion or an established spiritual tradition. There are many ways to work on our betterment and evolution outside the boundaries of strictly religious or spiritual endeavours.

A brutish, selfish and cruel human being who is a slave to their physical urges, their chaotic emotions and fear-based thought patterns will not qualify to step on the path of spiritual initiation. A person who mindlessly goes through life in ego unconsciousness, content to confine themselves to practical material living concerns, and enslaved to their established behavioural programming and comfort-seeking needs, will also rarely be ready to face the upward ascent of the spiritual path. The next evolutionary step for such a person is to start from where they are at and prioritise the desire to become a better person, and make more conscious choices rather than living as an automaton controlled by their programming. This desire to self-improve, if nurtured and maintained, will fuel a forward movement towards the refinement of their character. The attention on making more conscious choices rather than simply reacting to life based on emotional or psychological patterning is another key aspect of the uphill journey out of complete ego unconsciousness. Whether this is done with religious or spiritual intention, or simply as an act of intelligent living, is irrelevant. Eventually, the evolving human on this journey of self-betterment will inevitably reach up and out towards something greater than himself. This may be a desperate extension towards some cultural idea of God, or towards un unnamed sense of the Universe, or a greater intelligence, or even simply one's idea of 'Life'. The desire to consciously evolve into a better version of ourselves, combined with the search for a subjectively felt Transcendence, is what sets our feet on the probationary stage to the spiritual path. The process can be slow, or quite sudden, but at this point the unconscious human becomes an aspirant.

The Probationary Stage of the Aspirant

After eons of time spent spiritually unconscious and entombed in matter, a Soul has developed and prioritised their desire to become a better person and attempted to overcome the inertia of their patterning to make conscious choices according to moral values. They have evolved enough to have refined their character somewhat, and are now seeking some form of reconnection to the transcendent. The work done so far and their search for meaning will begin to attract the attention of their Soul. This pull towards the spiritual may manifest in a myriad of ways: an interest in religion, or philosophy, or seeking spiritual meaning through reading and study, or other forms of inquiry and experimentation into a more spiritualised, harmonious and unified way of living. Not everyone who is an aspirant feels called to religion, and not everyone who is a member of a religion is a spiritual aspirant. If one is a member of their religion because it is family tradition and expected of them, then it may not be as the result of a genuine calling and readiness for the path. Some people adopt a spiritual tradition because of the fear of a vengeful God and afterlife punishment, and some join their tradition because of a desperate need for belonging or wanting to feel special or 'chosen'. Partaking of religious practices out of fear, self-righteousness or simply because of obeying social or genetic programming is not the same as choosing the path from a place of genuine seeking for higher Truth and unification with the Divine.

At the probationary stage, the aspirant must pass three important tests in order to be admitted to the Spiritual Path proper:

- The test of recognition: the aspirant must be able to recognise his calling towards the spiritual path. The aspirant must be able to feel, respond to and recognise this call back towards his or her higher self, towards Spirit, towards God. This may be experienced as religious, or simply humanistic, but will always include the yearning for and orientation toward spiritualised values and qualities. If there is a calling to a particular faith, tradition or teacher, the aspirant must be able to recognise this as the "right" path or "right" teacher for them.

- The test of boundaries: Here the aspirant must hold firm and clear boundaries with all the things within himself, and all the things and people outside of herself, which may try to divert from embarking on the spiritual path. This may include other people's egos, judgment and fear (including the apparently well-meaning ones), naysayers and one's own fear-based egoic resistance. The aspirant must hold strong boundaries against this resistance and fear so he or she can stay the course directing them towards the spiritual path.

- The test of Discernment: The aspirant then must be able to recognise genuine spirituality, and genuine spiritual love, versus the fake spirituality and pretend love of false prophets. This is the aspirant proving that he can recognise the calling and the true spiritual path when he or she encounters it, by trusting the knowing of his soul, rather than the appearance of those of fair words and fair face. There will always be tempting offers trying to discourage or divert the path of the probationer, who must see them for what they are and stay true to the highest calling.

The Elemental Initiations

As this desire to become a better person drives the aspirant to make conscious uplifting choices aligning to self-improvement, and as they pass the 3 probationary tests, they eventually step onto the early phases of the spiritual path proper. At this stage the aspirant becomes a Disciple. The first four initiations on the Path are also called the elemental initiations because each of them is about mastering the energies of the four lower bodies: Physical, Emotional, Mental and Buddhic. Each of these first four levels corresponds to the energy of one of the four elements: fire for the first initiation, water for the second, air for the third and earth for the fourth.

Progress through the lower initiations also causes the gradual activation of the full set of seven human chakras, which are the energetic vortices of energy enabling the Soul Extension to communicate with and control the lower three vehicles. These seven chakras are commonly known these days. They are located at the base of the spine (root), in the area between the navel and the pubic bone (sacral), in the area of the stomach and liver (solar plexus), in the centre of the chest (heart), at the base of the throat (throat), on the brow (Ajna or brow) and at the top of the head (crown). At the completion of the third initiation, culminating in Soul Merge, the disciple has activated all seven of these chakras and downloads the next set of chakras. In the fourth initiation, the disciple integrates and activates these other 9 chakras, making up a total of fifteen active chakras. Some of these chakras are extension of or replacement for the previous seven as Soul Merge causes the descent of the three lower chakras into the Earth. Not all of the new charkas are located over the physical-etheric body however, as some will be in the aura, or further up or down the central energetic column running through the system of the disciple. This includes the Grounding Star located about six inches under the feet, and the Soul Star about six-inches above the crown.

Once the disciple moves into the higher initiations, they continue gradually loading and activating a large number of chakras, which work as part of the interfacing and functioning of the higher light-bodies that the initiate anchors and activates with each of the higher initiations.

The First Initiation

The first initiation is the fire initiation, because it involves the igniting of the Soul flame in the new disciple: a quickening of the body-mind awakening to the influence of the Soul's energy. The first initiation requires the disciple to develop mastery over the physical urges, fears and responses inherited from our primal animal ancestry. The first initiation disciple must free himself of the control of primal urges, instincts, and primal fear on the physical plane, so that he no longer is a slave to his physical existence. This includes overcoming the instinctive need to panic in the face of potential danger, showing the ability to grip one's body away from the fight-flight-freeze system in favour of consciously chosen responses to the situation. Mastery on the physical plane also includes the ability to function well on the physical plane, to care for one's physical well-being and survival, in order to support spiritual growth. We must all make a living, and do our best to be healthy, but part of mastering the first initiation is to do all this from a place of positive motivation and intelligence, love and wisdom, rather than from survival fear, selfish ambition or vanity. Another key areas of first initiation mastery is sexuality. One must not be a slave to their sexual desire, nor must they be completely in judgment of sex. Sex must be a conscious choice to express and share love. Everything that is done on the spiritual path must be done in love and in the service of one's spiritual growth and spiritual work, not in the service of lower egoic needs and desires. Each of the first three initiations is the process by which Soul gains control of the lower vehicle, so physical mastery means that the Soul is driving one's choices and behaviours on the physical plane. Manifesting the material means to achieve one's spiritual goals is part of physical mastery, and involves a spiritualised relationship to success, money, physical experience and health. The disciple must also be able to enjoy Earth life without being driven by hedonism. To complete the first initiation, the first degree disciple must raise their light quotient to be 35%.

The Second Initiation

The second initiation is the water initiation because it involves the mastery and refinement of the emotional nature, which is a lot like water in its fluidity and changing nature. The disciple must no longer be a slave to their emotions or their lower, selfish desires. This means many things, including the development of emotional intelligence: the ability to notice the ebb and flow of their own emotions and to identify those emotions appropriately. Not being controlled by our emotions is difficult if we are not consciously aware of them! The ability to notice and discern emotional currents in other people is also part of emotional intelligence. Emotional mastery means no longer being at the mercy of the chaotic and uncontrolled tides of emotions, but also not being in denial or avoidance of them. As long as we are human, we will experience emotions. The process of emotional mastery comes out of the realisation that we have emotions, but we are not our emotions. When we get triggered into certain emotions, we identify with the experience of that emotion and believe we are that emotion. We buy into the reality which usually comes with the emotions, instead of remaining as the in-dwelling Soul consciously choosing to respond to life rather than reacting from emotional impulse. The goal is to be emotionally present and engaged but not emotionally attached. This involved detachment is different from emotional absence and is a hallmark of emotional mastery.

Beyond emotional control, the second initiation demands a high degree of emotional purification. As explored in the last chapter section about the emotional body, there are lower and higher emotions. The goal of emotional purification is to release and transcend the predominance and control of negative emotions like anger, jealousy, fear, selfishness and hatred, and to reorient one's experience and expression towards higher emotional states and expression like affective warmth, kindness, joy or gratitude, for instance. Lower emotional states resist Soul control and lower our vibration, while higher emotional states are loving and uplifting energies which help raise our vibration. The other side of the coin is that the disciple must equally transcend the dependence on positive, pleasant emotions. This is where the feel-good addicts struggle. Chasing emotional highs -wanting to feel "good", warm and fuzzy, or excited all the time- is just as out of balance and dysfunctional are being under the thumb of constant negative emotions. Such an addiction is about needing the rush and relief that higher emotional states bring. Like any addiction, it is simply a symptom masking deeper unresolved issues. Why would one need to seek a sense of emotional comfort and relief if there was nothing to get relief from? People who always seek that form of emotional distraction must learn to recognise that these are signs of underlying wounding not being properly felt, acknowledged, and accepted. The same goes for those who are emotionally restless or erratic, like they can't wait to crawl out of their skin. If you are like that, ask yourself what you are trying to run away from? If you have some unresolved issue masked by such unrest and need for feel-good relief, then the wise way forward is to face the underlying issues, probably with some help, and resolve them. Only by facing our unresolved emotional tangles can we transcend their hold over us. Distracting yourself with dopamine rushes and co-dependent emotional attachments is not the masterful way.

Life is made of ups and downs; this is part of the mechanism through which we evolve. We learn both through pain and through joy, the agony and ecstasy of living. The fine balance point of emotional mastery is to not be controlled by our emotions (positive or negative) while still feeling and acknowledging our human emotional experience, whatever it may be. To deny negative emotions or suppress positive emotions is not a sign of mastery, but a sign of being afraid to experience emotions. A soul travelling the spiritual path must learn to welcome, feel and move through both extremes of the swings of emotional experience, yet not be under their control, not lose themselves in it or become consumed by them. Emotional triggers are not what motivate our decisions and actions, yet we are open to feeling the full range of human emotions. Second degree disciples learn how to move through, learn from and process emotions in healthy and growthful ways. In the end, they always realign their chosen resulting state towards one of more love, peace, wisdom, balance and harmony. Self-mastery means that the self – the indwelling soul animating this body - is the master of one's energy, experience, behaviour, choices and actions. On each level of the elemental initiations, the disciple must demonstrate that they can regain Soul control and be the master of their own self, on all levels of their energy system. In the process of mastering their emotional experience, one also learns to refine one's emotional nature and expression. I am sure we can all feel, intuitively if nothing else, that to be closer to God means experiencing less anger, hatred, shame and worry, and more love, hope, gratitude, calm and kindness. Therefore, as one learns to not be controlled by their emotions, and as they follow the natural inclination of their heart and soul nature, they will organically gravitate towards higher vibrational, balanced and peaceful emotional states. The disciple therefore refines and purifies their emotional nature to become more naturally, more often, in a more positive emotional bandwidth. Part of this emotional purification and refinement is the refining of the desire nature. Desire has a very strong emotional component. Selfish desire is a deep, strong emotional yearning in service of the fear-based, selfish ego. Such desire leads us to want something so badly that we prioritise the fulfilment of our desire over what is right, what is healthy or what is for the good. This form of lower need is all about 'me, me, me', the ego, what I want, what I need. Since it serves the negative ego, it is usually about the search for pleasure, or for avoidant relief from unresolved pain, regardless of the cost. As long as one is a slave to one's selfish desire nature, they cannot be in mastery of their emotional experience, nor can they be trusted to make wise and moral choices. The second-degree disciple must learn self-control, discipline, proper use of reason, and reorientation of one's choices and priorities towards the good and right, even if our little negative ego does not get its desperate selfish desires fulfilled. Be careful of the lies and stories we tell ourselves about why it is perfectly okay for us to pursue our selfish desires, regardless of cost or harm to ourselves, our eternal wellbeing, or the highest good of all concerned. Often, the ego likes to weave pretty little stories, create excuses, or justify why it is okay to stay locked in the cycle of desire addictions. Self-honesty is key in breaking through our own lies and stories.

It is important to note that at this point in the initiation process, the disciple still experiences conflicting and lower emotional states; this is simply human life happening of course! Yet, as the soul nears the completion of the second initiation, negative emotional states are much less a frequent feature of their experience. When she or he experiences negative emotions, the disciple does not indulge or wallow for long, but process them instead as they choose to realign their state towards higher ideals. One might say that the disciple's emotional diet becomes much healthier, and their emotional orientation more disciplined and ethical. In this process of emotional purification and refinement, the disciple raises their overall vibration again, inviting another dose of ascending-descension of one's soul energy, which produces a higher level of light present in the embodied vehicle. To complete the second initiation, the disciple must also reach a light quotient of at least of 45%.

The Third Initiation

This is the first proper initiation, in that it produces a tangible transformation in the energy system of the disciple. In actuality, the first three initiations are simply steps towards the completion of the third initiation, which culminates in the experience of Soul Merge.

The third initiation is the air initiation, which is the quick-moving element of the mind, thought, the intellect and inspiration. After developing some mastery on the physical and emotional levels, the next step for the evolving soul is to develop and refine one's mental nature, to master the mind. This involves quite a few different things, of which the nurture and development of the intellect is an important, but altogether small part.

At this level, one must one develop their intellectual capacity and mental intelligence, which are actually two different things. Developing one's intellectual capacity is basically a matter of developing mental skills and learning to make good use of the tool that is the intellect. Acquiring knowledge is but one part of this. Learning how to think and effectively apply one's mind to a variety of tasks, including mental deduction, discernment and analytical insight are all part of mastering the mind. The development of true intelligence is, however, a separate matter to that of simply learning how to drive the mental vehicle. Intelligence is more than performing clever mental tricks and knowing stuff. True intelligence is born out of a degree of illumination of the mind, which comes from allowing our thinker-mind to be illuminated by the knowing of the heart and of the Soul. One not only knows how to think, un-think, question, deduct, but is also receptive to the Soul's wisdom and light. The disciple must align to the higher mental pursuit of truth, its understanding and its application. This involves loving the truth above one's own existing beliefs and mental programs. It means nurturing an inquisitive mind and the capacity to be both open-minded and mentally discerning. For all this to happen, one must not be a slave to one's pre-existing beliefs and dogma but be willing to change their mind, be proven wrong, so as to learn and grow by using wise and intelligent mental evaluation of what is apprehended.

The disciple cannot genuinely achieve such mental skills and illumination without mental discipline. This means gaining conscious control of what we do with our mind. The disciple must be able to change their mind and change their beliefs at will. They can marshal their mental focus towards wise and desirable outcomes (this is much of what the 'power of manifestation' theory so popular in the new age is about), and eventually the capacity to generate their own new and illumined ideas and understanding. The hardest part of mental control for many is the quieting of mental noise and chatter. Every person has a voice in their head with which they talk to themselves, narrate their own experience, or judge and critique everything which is happening. It may in moments be useful to talk to yourself as you run through a to-do list for the day, or rehearse information you are trying to remember. But the voice that narrates or critiques everything is simply an aspect of the fear-based ego processing your reality. Remember that the conscious thinking mind is still part of the egoic personality structure. If you go around thinking your way through life, you are basically living as an egoic personality. If you go around forming opinions and judging everything, you are just being an ego. The soul experiences through feeling. We must learn to quiet the mind at will to create space within ourselves for the Soul. We must move our self-focus away from the head, and into the heart. As we centre in our hearts and feel our way through life, we set our feet on the path to Soul reality.

The third-initiation development of mental skill, intellectual capacity, illumination, intelligence, truth-seeking and mental mastery is both a precursor to and a consequence of the Soul taking progressive control of the mind. All three of the first initiations are in fact a process of the indwelling soul gradually taking control of each of the densest bodies: physical, emotional and mental. The soul is the level of self, and the vehicle, which resides on the Buddhic plane. The Buddhic plane is a sub-plane of the mental plane which is above the level of the lower mind, and therefore vibrates at a purer level. If the embodied body-mind part of us is the leaf, Soul is like the little branch upon which we grew. To gain control of the lower vehicle, the vibration of the lower vehicles has to be refined enough that the soul can interface with them. At the same time, the soul reaches into the levels of those lower vehicles to gain more control. As it does, it also brings its current levels of light, love and Knowing into those vehicles.

The completion of the third initiation marks the level whereby the Soul Extension has regained enough control and vibrational affinity with all three of the densest vehicles that the Soul can actually ground into them. The first three initiation are the progressive ascension of the lower vehicle into higher vibrations of expression, while the Soul gradually anchors its love, light and Knowing into the lower bodies and the Earth plane. At the completion of the third initiation, the disciple must have achieved a light quotient of 56%. The completion of the third initiation constitutes what is known as the first significant initiation, which is Soul Merge.

Soul Merge is the point whereby the soul vehicle and energy grounds into the physical, emotional and mental vehicles. As the Soul Extension descends, part of the personality structure–including the three lower chakras–is returned to the Earth and replaced with the Soul Extension's energy. From this point on, the soul basically replaces what was previously the separate human personality, which must be relinquished and returned into the earth to complete the transformation. The completion of the third initiation marks a noticeable shift in the disciple, who is now properly en-souled: holding a soul presence here now, in their embodied form. The human vehicle is still just human, but has now become a grounding focus and vessel for the Soul's energy to express and radiate. The disciple is more spiritually conscious and the difference can be seen in their eyes, like they (as a Soul) are more "there" now.

A word of warning for all and any disciples or initiates: regardless of where a spiritual traveller has achieved to in the initiation process, one can always fall back into unconsciousness if they make too many choices of fear, separation, ego identification, selfishness, cowardice or any negative ego expression. Even if one has completed the third initiation and Soul Merge, and should therefore express as the Soul embodied, all it takes if for them to get caught up in and identified with their lower egoic construct and old personality is for them to drop the soul identification and re-energise a sense of separate identity self again. Unresolved issues and feelings will continue to arise in the phenomena of the lower bodies, but we must approach them with a degree of witness consciousness so we can process them identified as the in-dwelling Soul. This is not about being disconnected from our feelings; the in-dwelling Soul must fully feel all there is to be felt. Indeed, the Soul lives through feeling. Feeling is a deeper and more expansive experience than just emotions. Feeling is the combination of physical sensations, emotions, mental and Soul experience all wrapped up in one. We must, however, remain identified as the Soul who is having a body-mind experience, but not identify with the feelings. The moment we get really triggered into what we are feeling, caught up in the reality and stories of our feeling experience, we become identified with that part of us. We lose Soul perspective and can no longer process what we feel. To come back to heart-centre and Soul identification is key. A useful mantra is to bring ourselves back:

"I have a body, yet I am not my body; I have emotions, yet I am not my emotions; I have a mind, yet I am not my mind"

It is crucial to note that anyone on the spiritual path, no matter how high they achieve, must continue to hold the expected standards of mastery and purity for their level of initiation. If they don't, they can fall down the top of the pyramid much faster than the time and effort it took them to climb it. While it is a lot of hard work to climb up the initiatory ladder, it is a lot easier to fall off it. It's a bit like a game of Snakes and Ladders. No one is who serious about spiritual achievement can rest on their laurels. High level initiates and Masters have less bandwidth for weakness and mistakes, not more.

The Fourth Initiation

This is the last of the elemental initiations, the earth initiation. It is associated with the element of earth because it requires us to fully ground Soul reality and release all earthly attachments in spiritual service. While the first three initiations were about mastering the lower three bodies, the fourth initiation is about mastering Soul reality, and the principle of Spiritual Intuition. Spiritual Intuition is the way the Soul guides itself, through the experience of Soul feeling and sensing, and includes the input and guidance coming from the Soul Tree. This is different from the primal guidance system of animal sensing and intuition, which has to do with registering subtle signals through the physical senses of smell, sight, touch, hearing and taste (like animals do). Navigating through life using our spiritual intuition rather than our thinker is a big shift, as it requires us to let go of what we think we know intellectually, and trust something more ineffable, yet deeper and real in our experience as a Soul. The disciple at this stage must also learn to consciously operate as a Soul independently from the body-mind, including on the inner planes of experience. The fourth-degree student must also actualise the knowing that energy and light are the same thing, and that therefore All is light.

After the experience of Soul Merge, the disciple is now grappling with living life as an embodied Soul, therefore meeting life through the eyes of unconditional love and the love of their fellow creatures. The essence of the Soul is to evolve and to love. This love gives birth to a service imperative within the disciple, who must now orient themselves more fully towards a very important aspect of travelling the spiritual path: spiritual service. The essence of the fourth initiation is the transcending of selfish personal attachment and personal desire in favour of selfless service. At this point, the evolving soul has merged and gained control of the lower three vehicles and is ready to start the work of making herself useful, in service to the greater Soul Tree that she is a part of, and in service to the Divine Plan. At this level, the embodied Soul disciple will be gradually inspired to make personal sacrifices in the service of a good cause, a higher love or a service mission. To complete the fourth initiation, the disciple must demonstrate that they can prioritise the greater good over their own personal interests, desires, attachments, personal beliefs, opinions and feelings. The everyday life of the fourth-degree initiate must be pervaded by their spirituality. The fourth initiation revisits all areas covered in the previous three initiations, and takes them to a new depth and degree of mastery. The disciple must be willing to give up every personal, earthly attachment in order to serve the greater good and the purpose of the Soul's spiritual work. This includes transcending the fear of death. This is why the completion of this initiation is often called the Crucifixion or the Renunciation. The initiate we now know as Jesus completed the fourth initiation on the cross, which was an amazing attainment at the time he served his spiritual mission. This particular Soul has now evolved way beyond the fourth initiation, of course.

Because the theme of personal sacrifice is central to this initiation, it is very important to understand the difference between pain and suffering. As we explored in the second initiation section, pain, like pleasure, is an inevitable part of life and an intrinsic aspect of the mechanism of learning and evolution here. The ability to face and welcome pain as life presents it to us, and to remain good and true in the face of it, is woven through the spiritual journey towards spiritual mastery. Part of how a soul evolves, becomes a proven spiritual initiate and eventually transforms into a spiritual Master, is in good part by demonstrating that we are able to remain true, good, clear, wise, ethical and steadfast in the light and love of Spirit even when faced with pain, loss, darkness or evil. Everyone begins by training to become a Master of self by demonstrating that we can remain steadfast in the love, light and truth of Spirit when facing our own darkness, fear, pain, inner demons. We must confront, clear and harmonise the evils in our own lives, as well as in our karmic baggage from other lives. This is us clearing up our own mess, created through the selfish, foolish and fear-based choices we made along the way as a Soul journeying through time. Once we achieve mastery of self, we train to become a working Master, whereby we must demonstrate the same ability in the face of the darkness, pain and evil present in the world. The working Master faces, purifies, vanquishes and illuminates darkness and fear on behalf of a greater good, in service to others, on whatever scale the master qualifies to work with. Handling the pain and challenge naturally present in life is therefore absolutely a part of the spiritual curriculum. Suffering, however, is a totally different concept. Suffering happens when we take the experiences presented to us, and create unnecessary pain for ourselves by choosing self-defeating attitudes and reactions. The Universal Mother and our own Soul Tree will present us with life experiences aimed at fortifying and fostering our growth and evolution. Some of them will be pleasant, some of them will be painful. How we react to and handle both is completely up to us; this is free will in an evolving system. We don't always consciously choose what happens to us, but we always have a choice about how we respond and what we make of it. We can take life in and turn it into anything we want: pain, fear, panic, joy, gratitude. A Master always takes life in and turns it into an array of flavours of love. Painful experiences can turn into great learning and food for transformation, just as pleasant experiences can. Every curse can become a blessing, and every blessing can become a curse, all depending on what we do with it. As they say, when life gives you lemons…. Suffering is a self-inflicted and unnecessary act of making things more difficult and more painful for ourselves than they need to be, by denying the gifts of evolution hiding within every experience.

Many people on the spiritual path confuse pain and suffering. They believe that making themselves miserable, depriving themselves needlessly, punishing themselves or making themselves suffer is going to ingratiate them to their God. This is the distorted glamour of the Martyr archetype, one which is very common particularly in those with a religious temperament. Didn't Jesus suffer for my sins? Then I must suffer too. Am I not supposed to prove my saintliness by making myself suffer? Does it make me holier to suck all the joy and fun out of life? This is, of course, a complete distortion and misunderstanding. God is about love, light and truth, not misery! The natural pain of life makes us stronger, while suffering makes us miserable. Accepting pain as part of the process of evolution means letting the Universe direct the process while we do our best to remain a presence of love, light and truth in the face of whatever presents. We must learn to welcome all the joy or pain life throws at us equally, as an opportunity to express our best spiritualised qualities. This is part of partnering with Spirit, as we trust Her benevolence and wisdom in giving us what we need to learn and evolve. In contrast, a paradigm of suffering is one where we decide to take matters in our own hands by manufacturing our own hardship through poor attitude and meanness towards ourselves. We believe that this suffering can serve as replacement for the divinely orchestrated difficulties that the Divine would otherwise provide for our learning. Yet, all this does is show ignorance of the ways of Spirit, and an addiction to pain. This is the misery-guts version of the Martyr archetype. A Soul generating their own suffering is not a bright soul of love, but a person locked in a cycle of self-torture, judgement, self-suppression and misery. None of these qualities are desirable in an impressive spiritual initiate. While the martyr archetype plays a role in the fourth initiation, there is a way to be a loving and even joyful martyr.

Love and joy being a martyr? Really? Yes. While sacrifice is a notion associated by most with a sense of agony, loss and torturous deprivation, it does not have to be this way… not if you approach it with the right mindset and attitude, and for the right reason. If you ask any good, loving parent whether they would be willing to sacrifice something very dear to them—or even themselves - in order to save their child, most would say yes. A good parent would gladly make many sacrifices in order to keep their child safe and well. This is what love does; it happily makes the necessary sacrifices in order to serve the object of their love. Sacrifice in service to a greater spiritual love is not different, simply more expanded in scope. The Martyr archetype is about sacrifice, but sacrifice is a necessary aspect of the process of change. If we want what is new, we must sacrifice what is old. If we want love, we must sacrifice fear. When we are ready and willing to move forward on the path, and we fully let go of all the attitudes and attachments of the previous stage of growth, the experience of sacrifice is graceful and fully embraced by choice.

Is it easy to make such radical sacrifices in the fourth initiation? No. Can it be challenging and painful? Yes. But we can still gladly chose it, knowing the rightness of it in our hearts, because we prioritise and value the greater love more than our own personal desires, attachments or needs…including to the extent of being willing to sacrifice our own life in service to the highest good of All. When we prioritise the love of God and the greater good above our little selves, a sort of transfiguration of the Soul occurs and we complete the fourth initiation. This initiation is called the Crucifixion experience, because like Jesus on the cross, the disciple must be willing to give up everything they own, everyone they are attached to, everything they desire and even in unto their own life, in selfless service to a greater good. These necessary sacrifices must be accepted and made peace with, because of one's love for their service mission. The disciple does not whine, or feel sorry for himself, like a self-absorbed little ego. Instead, they consciously choose this, regardless of their own personal feelings about it. They don't make it harder for themselves than it needs to be, and they don't create extra suffering in the process. The disciple love and support themselves through the process, they humbly accept what the higher call of Love demands of them and simply do what must be done. This is where many Hollywood hero movies go very wrong. I am sure we can all relate to having seen many a film where the hero finds himself in a position of being the one called to save the world…but oh no! He also has a family that he must save! All too often, the hero decides to save his family first, and only then goes and saves the whole world. Obviously, his one little family is so much more important than the entire world! Even ignoring the fact that the end of the world would automatically mean the end of his family - so, logically speaking, saving the world should probably be the priority - a true hero would never make the selfish choice of prioritising their personal attachment (family) over the higher calling to the greater good (world). This type of screenwriting caters to the sentimental sensitivities of an audience who are mostly nowhere near the completion of the fourth initiation, and would be upset to see the hero's family die, even if it meant endangering the entire world. The audience puts themselves in the hero's shoes, but everyone wants to be a hero without making the tough choices and necessary sacrifices that true heroism demands. This is another fallacy of the separate ego, who wants its cake and to eat it too. It is hard to understand the true selfless and impersonal nature of higher love when we are caught up in a lower love, which is about personal attachment and human sentiment. Movies are made mostly to entertain, so our screens are fully of stories where heroes are not real heroes.

The fourth initiation, leading to the crucifixion experience, is a major initiation and rite of passage for the evolving soul. It is the last of the 'lower' or elemental initiations, which focus on the mastery of one's own person and personal sphere. At this completion point, the in-dwelling soul finally demonstrates that they are loyal to the higher calling of Spirit first, before any considerations of their separate ego self or the egos of others. Regardless of the feelings and difficulties encountered as part of this transformational sacrifice, the disciple consciously chooses it in a self-determining manner because their whole existence is reoriented towards higher ideals of spiritual service.

What is spiritual service? Spiritual service is the activity we undertake to play our part, as guided by higher spiritual intelligences, to advance the goals and purpose of the Divine Plan. The very notion of spiritual service reconnects us to the ultimate truth that we are not separate islands in a sea of random matter, but a part of something much bigger. We all have a part to play, and a purpose to fulfil. If Creation was an engine, each of us would be the small parts and cogs within that engine. In order for the engine to function properly, each little screw, part, cylinder and cog must fulfil their function and play their part. When certain things malfunction and stop doing what they are supposed to do, the engine struggles and can even break down altogether. A system where too many parts don't function according to their original intended design will be a system in a state of degradation and breakdown. As above, so below...Every organ and cell in our bodies have a particular design, role and function. When organs or even individual cells stop functioning as they are supposed, according to their original biological design and function, we have illness. This planet is an organ within our solar system, and our solar system is a larger organ within this galaxy. System malfunction is our current situation on this planet, where too many human souls are mired in unconsciousness, serving their own separate egos, and oblivious to their belonging and responsibility to the greater Being that they are a part of. The environmental damage, ill health, destruction, war, violence, greed and corruption we see are part of the dysfunction here. The collective of Humanity, spiritually unconscious and consumed by the quest to fulfil their selfish needs and ambitions, is causing evolutionary harm and disease by living in disharmony with the greater Whole that we are a part of. Narcissistically convinced of their separate and independent existence, and of their entitlement to do and take whatever they want, humans are slowly degrading themselves and their environment. There are some bright lights, mind you, but they are a minority. Higher levels of Creation consider our epidemic of negative ego a form of spiritual illness, which needs to be healed and brought back into a state of health. This is where lightworkers come in, who are like the spiritual immune response of this system. Lightworkers are the disciples and initiates spiritually awake enough to remember that they are part of a larger system, and willing to do their bit to help restore health and harmony on this beautiful little planet. Many lightworker Souls projected into incarnation at this time in Earth's history; sadly many of them have not answered the call to service, distracted by the glamours and comforts of our modern civilisation. Lightworkers have the difficult task of attempting to realign our current state of affair towards the evolutionary ideals of harmony, unity, balance, peace and wisdom. Like immune cells, lightworkers have a variety of possible roles and functions, including the destruction of illness-producing elements, the embodying and modelling of ideal healthy cell function, and the rebuilding and restoration of natural health processes. This is spiritual service. As part of this work, lightworkers provides levels of continued guidance and support to the evolving creature life wave here, so we can get back on track with desirable lines of evolutionary experience and exploration. Source's exploration and evolution cannot continue if Creation becomes sick and destroys itself before its time. Lightworkers are thoroughly needed in this world, at this time. Initiates of any degree, and all people, can choose to play a small part in the work of the healing. The fourth initiation represents a major transition in the initiate's life, whereby spiritual service becomes their overarching priority, their primary soul and life commitment. This transformation begins progressively, requiring moderate efforts and personal sacrifices in order to serve the good of others. As the disciple progresses, the initiation culminates in the Crucifixion or Renunciation experience, whereby the disciple proves they are willing and able to sacrifice all personal desires and personal attachments in service of the higher good.

As they go through this initiation, the disciple gradually enters a new state of consciousness called Flow, which features a different sense of time, space, cause and consequence. This is fourth-dimensional consciousness. Up to this point, third-dimensional consciousness was experienced, where we perceive our space-and-time environment as linear and concrete. In third-dimensional consciousness, objects are separate from us and each other; We must exert a certain amount of physical, emotional or mental force in order to make things happen. The experience of flow is the beginning of perceiving, in our real and felt experience, that space, time, cause and consequence are connected into a unified flow. It is the beginning of feeling interconnected-ness, and the early ability to manifest through intent and energy flow rather than the third-dimensional approach of pushing blocks of matter around.

The fourth stage disciple must also need to achieve a light quotient of 62% to complete the fourth initiation.
****

At the completion of the 4th-stage crucifixion experience, the lower elemental initiations are complete. The disciple now officially becomes called an initiate, rather than a disciple. While the first four initiations are referred to as the Spiritual Path, the higher initiations are the Path of Ascension. In the higher initiations, the Soul begins to activate light-bodies, which exist on the planes above the mental plane, and above where Buddhic soul vehicle resides. Light-bodies are much less dense that the lower bodies, and are made of various levels of Source light. As such, they provide a higher vibrational and expansive experience. Up to this point, the initiation process has been about the soul gaining control of the human vehicle, eventually merging with it, accessing spiritual guidance and inspiration, and dedicating itself fully and completely to playing its part within the Divine Plan. From here on, the higher initiations are when the Soul itself – i.e. one soul extension on the Oversoul Tree–expands her consciousness and identification to include and grow into a larger chunk of the Soul Tree. As it grows, the Soul progressively activates, integrates, expands into and becomes informed by more and more of the energy and Knowing of its Soul Tree. Spiritual service work is at this stage a fixture of the process. Most of these initiations involve the completion of service projects of increasing scope and effect as one progresses through each initiation.

Please bear in mind that it becomes harder to describe the experiences and transformations that higher initiates experience as they expand into planes, states of being and dimensions which are beyond the capability of the lower mind to truly grasp. Increasingly, the experience of the higher initiations becomes formless, timeless, multi-dimensional and ineffable. I will do my best to summarize some key points about each of these higher initiations, up to the 9th initiation which currently forms the completion of the planetary ascension. There is little point in exploring anything beyond this point as very, very few embodied souls on the planet have achieved to those levels on the ascension path (contrarily to many grand claims in the new age arena).

The Fifth Initiation
This is the first of what is called the higher initiations, and it results in the activation of the first of the higher

spiritual bodies: The Atmic body. The Atmic body is anchored, and then gradually awakened and activated as one successfully progresses through this initiation. Activation of the Atmic body allows us to be aware, conscious and acting on the Atmic plane, which is the lowest level of connection with Divine Will manifest. The dimensional quality of reality on the Atmic plane is Flow. The core essence of the fifth initiation is the mastery of Spiritual Will. It also begins the process of Soul integrating the energy of other incarnations of its Soul Group.

Now that the evolving soul has sacrificed their separate-self attachments in service to the Soul's purpose, the fifth initiation enables the beginning of feeling, sensing and aligning to Divine Plan, and aligning the Will of their Soul and body-mind to this Plan. This is the first contact of the individual Soul with the lowest flows of Divine Will as it flows through the Soul Tree's purpose. In the previous initiation, the Soul began to guide themselves, in service to All That Is, by their spiritual intuition. This intuition is now used to feel, sense and understand their part in the Plan and Will of God, and to wield their own Spiritual Will in its service. They must then demonstrate that they can express these beginnings of partnering with the Will of God by applying their own Spiritual Will selflessly in their service activities, in alignment with Divine Plan. It is a fine balance to use our spiritual will without imposing any personal agenda or ideology upon it. This is a different way of using will, which has nothing to do with the ego, and everything to do with allowing ourselves to be an extension of our Soul Tree, and the expression of the purpose for which we were created. We must learn to use our will in a way which is surrendered to and in service of Divine Will.

The fifth initiation is also the first truly major initiation because it is the point at which the individual

Soul extension is at the very beginning of expanding their consciousness into the reality of the larger Soul Tree being they are a part of. This is done through the integration of the energy of our Soul Group, Oversoul and beyond: a process called Soul braiding (when working at the level of the Group Soul and Oversoul) and Monadic braiding (working at the level of the Monad in later initiations). Although some degree of Soul braiding can begin in the fourth initiation, the fifth initiation is where the journey of Soul braiding becomes a large part of our process, as we integrate the energy and Knowing of our Soul group and Oversoul. Let me offer a nutshell explanation of what Soul braiding is. Since Soul is now expanding its consciousness and energy into its Soul lineage and Soul Group, it must now also absorb and refine the energy of all the other leaves on that branch. Each of the other leaves are expressions of the same Soul lineage and Group Soul energy, expressed in different physical embodiment through time and space. Yes, we are talking reincarnation, which I will explore further in the next chapter. As the ascending Soul becomes a vehicle for the Knowing of the branch, so do we realise and feel deeply that these other embodiments are also part of us, expressions of our energy in other places and times. This is more than a mental understanding; it is a truly tangible, deeply felt experience. Past life memories can surface at this point. Soul memories will generally come as feeling memories, for feelings are the language of the Soul. This differs from the conscious mental memories you may have from what has occurred in this current life. The conscious mind cannot remember other lives because this body-mind did not exist then! The Soul has its own way of remembering. More importantly, feelings from other lives present not just for fun; they come up to be addressed and refined, in the same way that the physical, emotional and mental experience from this life had to be faced, purified and refined to prepare this embodiment for the higher initiations. This is how we clear our karma, which is another feature of the initiation process. As you do the spiritual work, progress and become a successful embodiment of your Soul Tree's energy, then this embodiment also becomes a point of focus for purifying the energy and karma of other embodiments on your branch. Remember that everything is energy. Feelings are energy. Choices we make and intentions we hold set energy into motion. Everything a Soul has done, chosen and felt in other lives is part of the karma of the Soul branch of which we, as an individual embodiment, are but one leaf. In the elemental initiations, we processed through our own individual life energy from this incarnation, refined it to higher levels of light and love, and mastered our lower bodies so that the Soul part of us was in control. In order to continue ascending through the initiation process, we must do the same with everything we integrate and become one with. This includes all the energy of all the other incarnations of the same branch. We continue to refine and enlighten our energy, and raise our quotients of light, love and purity while identified as the branch, rather than just the leaf. As the ascending soul identifies as the branch, and welcomes and clears all the feelings from these other soul-leaves embodiments, the vibration of the entire ascending soul/branch is raised. The raising and purifying of our own four-body system continues in the higher initiations, but it expands to process the Soul Group energy that we are a part of and identify with. Clearing it means raising the energy of the totality of the branch's energy, including all its other incarnations. This is the beginning of raising our karmic balance throughout time, into more love. As we integrate more of our Soul Group branch, we integrate the learning, and the wisdom of whole branch becomes what we are informed by. This repeats in further higher initiations as the Soul integrate and becomes informed by the energy and wisdom of the entire Soul Group, and the Oversoul. Then it continues on to the Monadic level, which we could refer to as the Forest, in further initiations. Everything which is part of our Soul Tree must be purified, trained, refined and mastered in the same way as we did with our human vehicles in the previous initiations. The process is basically the same, but on a different scale. Part of the processing is the a realignment of the energy of other leaves so that the force vectors of all incarnations of that branch become committed to the same spiritual ideals as we hold now as the ascension vehicle. This process of integration, transmuting, purifying, aligning and integrating the energy of other soul extensions becomes a considerable and somewhat consuming part of the process in the higher initiations. By clearing the karma and refining the energy of these other embodiments, we integrate and are able to access their collective wisdom and Knowing. This is where the magic of being able to access greater Knowing, beyond the limited experience of this life, becomes possible.

As the initiate progresses through the fifth initiation, they also gradually embrace the state of fifth dimensional consciousness, which is Oneness.

To complete this initiation, the initiate must achieve a light quotient of at least 75%.

The Sixth Initiation

The sixth initiation marks the anchoring and gradual activation of the Monadic light-body, and is another major initiation. The Monadic presence energy is also called the Mighty I Am Presence. The Monadic light-body will be fully activated and expressed at the completion of the sixth initiation, which marks the achievement of what is called Ascension.

At this level, the process of soul braiding continues, and expands further into the process of Oversoul braiding, and the very early stages of Monadic braiding. This is the same process as soul braiding, but expanded into a vaster portion of the Soul Tree and some of the Monadic Forest's energy. Consequently, the energy of many more Soul branches and many more leaves must be felt, purified, aligned and integrated into a wholeness of presence, at a level of vibration meeting the requirements of the sixth initiation. The process of integrating the energy of so many more leaves in the Soul Tree means we become deeply engaged in processing and refining vast amounts of energy. This is very preoccupying and involves many waves and storms of feelings, each leading to the integration of more energy, and many shifts in vibration and expression. The individual soul expression changes at this level, as the individual Soul expression is added to and slightly altered by the integration of other leaves' energies and their knowing. The presence of the individual Soul is still there, but it also becomes more, and can be changeable depending on how much it draws on the energy and Knowing of the various branches of the Tree in different moments.

This initiation is about achieving a good mastery of Divine Intelligence. This is also the level of coming closer to a unified knowing of Divine Love. Where the fifth initiation was the beginnings of perceiving Divine Will and Divine Plan (further initiations take us deeper into this Knowing), the sixth initiation is the beginning of unifying with the omnipresence of Divine Love, and becoming a vessel for it through the expression and mastery of Divine Intelligence. Divine Love is a much higher vibration and expression than what most people call love, which is human love. It is also more than simply unconditional love. Human love is very personal and usually sentimental. Divine Love is completely unconditional and universal, radiant, and encompasses expressions such as gratitude, compassion, joy and mercy. It is a light-infused Love from All That Is to All That Is. It is bright and clear, not warm and fuzzy like the average person would expect love to feel. This is a form of enlightened love which illuminates the darkness, is a stark mirror and challenges fear. It is a love that nurtures not our little comforts, but our evolution. Divine Love is that which nourishes the evolution of All Life, but Divine Intelligence is what weaves and eventuates outcomes in order to nurture the evolution of All Life. The sixth-degree initiate learns to express through spiritually intelligent activity, in service of Divine Love.

Spiritual Intelligence is the intelligence of the Mind of God. It is wise; it is enlightened; it is adaptable; it is in service of evolution and the highest Good of All. Most people confuse being brain-clever with being intelligent. In spiritual terms, true intelligence cannot exist where one's intelligence is unenlightened or not in the service of higher love. Spiritual intelligence is illumined by God's light and the knowing of the pure heart, always. Any other types of "intelligence" is not really intelligence. The mastery of spiritual intelligence requires the capacity to use all levels of the Mind, including access to the higher mental planes of ideas, concepts and direct Knowing, in service of Divine Love. The initiate must be able to receive clear inspiration, understand in their Soul rather than their egoic mind, have analytical insight, deduct, implement, plan, strategise, adapt their perceptions and create, all from a place of Divine Illumination, wisdom and Divine Love, in service to All That is. This enables the ability to translate and put into practice the Divine Will and the Divine Plan, which the initiate began to grasp in the fifth initiation. Spiritual Intelligence is actualised when we can make things happens in the world, through our own illumined intelligence activity, as an expression of Divine Will and Divine Love.

Going hand in hand with this journey of becoming a vessel for Divine Intelligence in service of Universal Love, the initiate also enters fifth dimensional consciousness, which is the experience of Oneness. This is the organic progression from the fourth dimensional consciousness of Flow, whereby we experienced the interconnectedness of things and how they flow into each other. Oneness takes this one steps further in feeling and knowing that things are not only connected, but indeed All part of the Oneness of life. Objects, people, time, space, experiences all becomes various facets of the same Source and its one invisible matrix. All parts are expressions of an overarching greater One. This is not simply understood as an intellectual concept, but tangibly experienced, perceived and felt. The initiate experience themselves more and more as an intrinsic part of this oneness, bound to it in love, with love and by love. The higher and lower parts of the self become more unified, and our experience of time less linear as we begin to experience the Eternal Now. This is unity consciousness and is the beginning of holding an ascended consciousness.

To complete this initiation, the initiate must achieve a light quotient of at least 83%. The completion of the sixth initiation also marks the point where the initiate Soul is now liberated from the wheel of reincarnation. They are no longer karmically bound to the obligation of incarnating in order to harmonise their planetary karma. This is because in order to complete the sixth initiation, we must have processed, harmonised and refined the energy of our entire planetary karma to be at least 51% love. This means that all the energy this Soul has contributed to this planet through its choices and presence, over its entire chain of incarnations on Earth, must have been refined enough to have contributed more love than fear into the world. At this point in the initiation process, the Soul has the choice to either reincarnate, or not; and to either continue their progression in service on this planet, or leave Earth and continue their evolution elsewhere.

At the successful of the completion of the sixth initiation, the initiate is considered a junior Master on the planetary level.

The Seventh Initiation

The seventh initiation is a truly major and transformational initiation. Until as recently as a hundred years ago, the seventh initiation marked the completion of planetary initiation. This has now changed, as evolution progresses on every level of our Creation. Times are changing, and the planet is choosing to move into a new phase of her evolution. What constitutes the completion of the curriculum of evolutionary learning rises as the planet herself evolves. We are obliged to keep up since humanity is part of this planet. Although the seventh initiation is still considered part of the final stretch towards completing planetary ascension, full completion is now at the ninth initiation. The seventh initiation is, however, the last of the completion initiation to be experienced tangibly on the outer planes of form life. After the seventh, much of the transformation and change happens in the light-bodies and in one's inner experience. All the initiations–from the third and up–have at different times marked the culmination of spiritual evolution as pertaining to the planetary level of mastery. It is a positive sign to acknowledge that the spiritual goal-post moves up because the overall vibration and evolution of the whole planet is moving forward, despite the highs, lows and birthing pangs encountered along the way. Humanity is currently struggling to adapt to this planetary evolutionary decree. Every human soul currently has to choose whether to step up and adapt, or resist and become part of the problem. This is the long-prophesied "judgment day", which has little to do with judgment, and everything to do with a collective test and opportunity to move up the evolutionary spiral. Gaia, or planet Earth, is much more than a big rock upon which humanity exists. She is a living, sentient planetary being composed of a mineral kingdom (her skeleton), a plant kingdom (her organs), an animal kingdom (her emotional body), a human kingdom (her mental body) and a soul kingdom (her Buddhic body), and that is not counting the many elemental, systemic intelligences and natural forces which keep her system functioning. Humanity's resistance to the overall raising of vibration on a planetary level is partly responsible for the exacerbation of conflict and struggle we are currently witnessing around the world. Having more people spiritually wake up and consciously applying themselves to self-betterment and spiritual evolution is one of our greatest needs at this time in our history. We need more initiates dedicated to planetary service work to assist and facilitate this transition as smoothly as possible.

Regardless of the new completion point of planetary ascension, the seventh initiation remains a major transformation and reordering of the entire energy system or the initiate. The process of integrating the various soul branches of their Monad (Soul Forest) continues and picks up speed. This means processing, refining and integrating enormously vast amounts of energy in order to integrate and become one with the Knowing of the Monadic being which they, as an individual soul leaf, are a part of. Seventh-stage initiate consciousness evolves to become increasingly part of a Monadic collective. This is the beginning of Divine Illumination and Divine Awareness, as part of working with Life itself.

As the initiate journeys through the seventh stage, they anchor and gradually activate their Logoic body, learning to become more aware and active on the Logoic Plane, which is the plane where we experience Divine Grace and Is-ness. Is-ness is the complete absence of judgment and the transcending of duality. It is the end of perceiving life in opposites: good versus bad, right versus wrong, better versus worse. At the completion of this initiation, the initiate experiences everything simply as a complex tapestry of cause and consequence, neither good nor bad. It all simply is. Personal opinions and ideology become redundant. The initiate experiences an irrevocable Knowing that anything can in some contexts, be love… or just as easily not be. Absolutes no longer exists and a new simplicity qualifies reality. This demands all-encompassing acceptance and surrender, heart consciousness, as well as very high levels of purity and clarity on every level. Any area of competency achieved with minimum pass-marks in previous initiations get a serious revision to raise our marks at this initiation. No stone shall be left unturned! This initiation places our reality firmly into sixth dimensional consciousness (see Chapter 2).

After learning to master Divine Will in the fifth initiation, and Spiritual Intelligence in the Sixth, the seventh initiation facilitates the mastery of Divine Grace, and the beginning of working with Life itself. This is the next organic step in the journey of expansion of consciousness and ascension. Divine Grace is the result of returning to the Knowing present in the Mind of God. It is a stage of returning home, in spiritual terms. It can be experienced as an absolute, embodied knowing that "All is One, All is Love and All is Light", as we flow effortlessly with the currents of Divine Love which exist to nurture All evolution. The initiate feels an inexorable pull towards being a vessel of Divine Love, Divine Purpose and Divine Intelligence, and an ease in expressing it in service of the evolution of all they encounter. They become themselves a force of evolution, just by virtue of what they are. It becomes easier to be love than anything else. There is an irrevocability and effortlessness in this, which must be mastered at the seventh stage. This is not to say that the seventh-stage initiate will not encounter challenges or have to work hard in their service work, but the difficulties will not be in them. The seventh stager must successfully master equanimity, which is a natural and steady experience of a balanced calm and steady peace which is always there, at our core, even when we experience feelings and challenges in our lives. A new core anchors as a more eternal and impersonal sense of Self. As the Logoic body fully activates, it forms a protective shell of golden light, which helps maintain the clarity and purity of the energy which is held within the initiate's field of presence.

Beyond this, the initiate begins relating with Life itself, which transcends both Love and Light. It is a difficult reality to explain to those who have not experienced it, but seventh-stage initiates are in the beginning stages of partnering with Life through the mechanism of Divine Awareness. As the seventh-stage initiate begins to partner with Life, they experience the early dimensional consciousness of co-creation with the Divine plan of evolution. They also become more actively and expansively involved in service work on a planetary scale, and the Logoic body is large enough to contain the entire planet within the aura of the realised seventh stage Master. To complete this initiation, we must achieve a light quotient of at least 92%.

Much of the inner life of the initiate (i.e. their experience on the higher planes) changes and expands greatly. The huge expansion of consciousness experienced at this stage grows to include levels and realms encompassing not only the entire planet but also touching into perceiving at the solar levels, and sometimes beyond peeking into galactic level. Not all initiates develop or display the same abilities, so the extent of this can vary. In addition, being able to perceive higher realities is not the same as being conscious and active on those levels. This process will continue to unfold in the eighth and ninth initiations.

The Eighth and Ninth Initiations

At the time of writing this book, hardly anyone has achieved the eighth and ninth initiations while embodied in a physical body. A tiny number of master-souls existing on the inner planes (i.e. on planes of existence encompassing the higher mental plane and above) have achieved to those levels on this planet. It is therefore pointless to explain these higher initiations in too much details.

Through the eighth and ninth stages of initiation, the evolving Soul experiences this part of their journey much more within their inner reality than on the outer planes of manifestation. At this level, we anchor and activate the Group Soul body (8th initiation) and Group Monadic body (9th Initiation), and activate our consciousness on the Co-Creator levels. This is where we learn to work in full unified Co-Creation with Divine Will, Divine Love and Life itself to carry out the Divine Plan. The consciousness of this stage of evolution is Co-Creator consciousness, which is Pure Awareness as the initiate begins to experience Oneness with Source itself.

As the name suggest, here we more fully surrender to becoming a part of and a vessel for the various evolutionary forces we partner with. We become a marked influence on the process of evolution on this planet, and by the end of the ninth initiation, our Will becomes fully integrated not only with the Will of the Monad, but also with planetary purpose. Awareness expands into the solar and galactic levels, while just being able to perceive realms of the universal and cosmic levels of Creation. Remember, however, to being able to perceive on such levels is not the same as being a conscious participant. The experience of transcendent Joy becomes a feature of these levels, although it is not the type of joy that most human beings would expect. This joy is anchored in a deep equanimity, and is simply a result of being completely at one with the Knowing of the benevolence of our Divine Creation and Creator.

To complete planetary ascension at these levels, the initiate must achieve a light quotient of 99.9%. It is impossible to get a full 100% light quotient, because this is a free-will system. In order to enable the use of free will, Soul must have more than one thing to choose from. If light is all there is, then free will becomes redundant. The free-willed Soul must have a seed of potential darkness and fear within itself in order to have the potential for choice, which makes free will possible.

The fully actualise planetary ascension, the initiate must also complete a planetary bestowal, which is like the final practical exam within the context of planetary service. A planetary bestowal can be completed anytime between the end of the seventh initiation and the completion of the ninth. This important service project must be something which alters the gross destiny of the planet, in harmony with evolutionary goals and the Divine Plan, and which would not have happened without the intercession and work of the initiate in question.

****

The evolutionary initiation process does not end here. The ninth initiation is currently ascension on the planetary level only, but we know there is a whole

Cosmos out there, waiting to be expanding into! By the time they complete planetary ascension, the local Master Soul is long freed of karmic ties and obligations towards this planet (freedom from the wheel of karma occurs at the end of the sixth initiation). As a Master reaches the pinnacle of initiation on this planet, they again have a choice: remain active on this planet to serve and support the process of evolution here, or move on to other planets and spheres to continue their evolution in other worlds. There are 352 initiations in total to get to the level of full return to oneness with Source. Reaching the top initiations of the planetary process is quite an impressive and still rare achievement within the context of our little blue sphere, yet it represents but kindergarten kid's play within the greater scheme of solar, galactic, universal and cosmic evolution.

This journey of initiation is one that every evolving Soul will undergo at some point or another within the span of their eternal existence. None can avoid it, because we are all but part of a much, much larger Being, who directs our overall evolutionary direction, just as our brain directs our nervous system. Most, as human leaves on our Soul Tree, simply suffer from momentary spiritual amnesia. We have forgotten that we are but the leaves at the end of the branches of the spirit trees that populate the infinite forest of Divine Creation. We are all creations, expressions and children of God, of Source, of the Great Spirit of All. When we begin to search again for our true origins, and our true nature, then we are just beginning upon the journey back to full spiritual memory of who and what we are.

CHAPTER 4

The Wheel of Reincarnation

~~~

The sense of having forgotten something, forgotten who and what I was, or why I was here, was what drove me to look for more. As a fifteen-year-old, I could not clearly articulate even to myself what I felt was so missing in my life. All I knew was that the picture the world offered me was incomplete, although I could not remember what was missing. The spiritual amnesia of everyone around me seemed ever worse than mine! Not only had they forgotten, like me, who and what they were and what life's true purpose was... but they had forgotten that they had forgotten!

And so, in my own way, I began searching. I started searching for a sense of greater purpose, driven by that need to contribute something worthwhile to my world, to give back or help somehow. I wanted to find something that made my heart sing while also being useful within the context of something greater than myself. This search was what propelled me into the early stages of my spiritual journey of initiation. My feelings at the time were deep, rising like tidal waves on a daily basis. None of what I felt could really be explained by the mundane happenstance of my 20th century adolescent self, but it could not be denied. Tides of feeling came daily to be experienced, sometimes cried out, occasionally silently screamed (on the inside) and released. I did not understand what was happening to me: why was I feeling so much, so intensely? Other teenagers around me did not have the same experience. Why was I constantly filled with yearning for an unknown? Others seemed happy enough just bobbing along. Whether I understood it or not, it became how my life was: the normality of school, teen friends and parents, bathed in the strangeness of deep, apparently timeless feelings and the pull of the invisible hand towards what I had forgotten.

Music proved to be a supportive companion throughout those adolescent years. It helped me flow with the many feelings that were surfacing, supporting a sort of catharsis. Because music had become such a healing influence in my life, I decided I wanted to become a famous musician. Perhaps I too could make music to move people's hearts and heal their souls? Perhaps I too could, through music, express the invisible and ineffable things that sought to be remembered and known from behind the veil of my consciousness? The arts can be such a vehicle for feeling, healing, inspiration and transformation, if done right. Art done "right"? What does that mean? Looking at it within a context of our great evolutionary journey, doing art "right" is when the act of creation is approached not as a narcissistic dumping ground of thoughts and emotions, but as a transformative way of expressing the wonder and horrors of the human condition. Artistic expression should be a service to our audience, not a self-indulgent wallowing. Only when approached as a service can art be truly transformational and inspirational. For a little while, as a young seeker, I thought that this was an avenue for my future. While the career in music was ultimately not my path, it was a precious contributor to the early phase of my healing and growth. It provided support for the processing of many unresolved feelings and issues over the years of my adolescence and early adulthood. Regardless of these many gifts in healing and self-exploration, music was not giving me the answers I sought. I still felt cast at sea in my life; I was still searching for a place to anchor my ship.

I ended up in a bookshop, on a rainy summer's day in New York City; I was twenty years old. I and my boyfriend ran into the nearest bookshop for shelter from the pelting rain, as we both loved to read. Shaking the raindrops off our hair and clothes, we walked past a wall with shelves proudly displaying a countdown of New York Times bestselling books through the years. One of those books was "The Mists of Avalon" by Marion Zimmer-Bradley. The cover proudly displayed the mythical image of an ancient priestess riding a white horse amongst a misty, timeless landscape, a sword held ceremoniously in her hands.

"You should buy this book." my boyfriend said, pointing to the priestess on her white horse. "You'll love it. It's full of hocus-pocus."

Hocus-pocus…. this soon became his blanket name for the spiritual topics this book would lead me to grow interested in. Like many people who are not seeking, content in their spiritual amnesia, he saw my spiritual interest as a harmless yet somewhat silly, irrational quirk. Many spiritual aspirants surrounded by non-spiritual, unawakened people face similar reactions. Those who are fully content to define their existence within the realm of the body-mind can mock, or at least be dismissive of, those who search for what is beyond. They assume it is a modern form of medieval hocus-pocus superstition (you know, before we had things like reason and intelligence!), or simply the act of desperate people madly grasping for something to make them feel better about their sad little lives. To be honest, these assumptions are not without foundation. I have met both these types of pseudo-spiritual seekers: those riddled with fear who cling to the spiritual like a charm that will keep them safe; and those who seek not truth, but comfort and certainty in a world which provides very little of either. I can therefore understand why the non-spiritual make such assumptions, having never themselves experienced the call and yearning of the Soul for its metaphysical home. I did not mind this hocus-pocus name calling. I felt what I felt. Whether he or others understood mattered little; this was too important for me to care what others thought about it. I am still, to this day, grateful to him for pushing me to buy that book, because the reading of it would offer the next step in my spiritual quest.

Stories have power. Story-telling has been used to embed and remember our history, our culture, convey moral lessons and to take people on subjective journeys of feelings, ideas and knowing, in a way that few other cultural tools can. A well-crafted story, produced by a genuinely inspired and service-oriented artist, can become a vehicle for healing and transformational magic for the receptive reader. In those early adult years, I began reading more avidly of both fiction and non-fiction. Some people read to escape their lives, which may not be helpful as it can encourage avoidance and denial of one's responsibility towards reality. But there is another approach to reading. I learnt that a good book could be like a mirror: to help me reflect on certain topics, to see my own feelings and reactions mirrored in the story or information shared. A good story moves you. New information can challenge you. Regardless of the words on the page, the feelings and thoughts you have about the book are still completely yours. Because of the response it generates in you, a book becomes a useful mirror by which you can observe yourself, learn about your reactions and feelings, wonder about the layers of your inner ocean being exposed, and so learn a little more about yourself. I knew this magic and used reading as part of my self-exploration, just as I had done with music. Reading "The Mists of Avalon" was a whole new experience. I laughed, I cried but also, somehow, I remembered what the story was describing. It was not the actual story of King Arthur, Merlin, Guinevere and Morgaine that I remembered, of course. But the times, culture and spiritual traditions which form the background of this story echoed of something I knew at Soul level. It was nothing like the distinct memories we may have of our last birthday or our first kiss, but I felt like I remembered ancient Britain. I remembered riding on horses for many hours, sometimes in the rain with my cloak soaked, until finally finding shelter and warmth at an inn. I remembered stone castles and the coldness of their corridors. I also remembered the type of loss described in the story, painfully so, although I had never experienced it in this life. And most of all, I remembered the general feeling of the ancient mystical spiritual traditions of the Celtic lands. I read the book three times in a row, until I was done with the process this book was taking me through. The next day, I went to the bookshop, and bought my first spiritual self-help book: one on the magic of herbs and crystals.

I will add a comment here about an important mental orientation everyone should have when engaging with fiction stories, be it in books or movies. Remember that as far as your subconscious and the Soul are concerned, everything you feel is real, and therefore a reality. If you engage with a fictional story, which makes you feel things, and get carried away into the story like it's your reality, the Soul will begin to upload those fictional experiences as real, and therefore inscribe them as part of your Soul karmic flows. This is why it is key, before watching a movie or reading a novel, to always instruct your mind and yourself as a Soul to know and remember that the story you are engaging with is not real, and it's not happening to you. Remind yourself of this throughout.

Reading "The Mists of Avalon" opened a new door for me, the door of Soul remembrance. This was my official, conscious, first step on the spiritual path. I sneaked a proper peek behind the veil of my spiritual amnesia and remembered something of my Soul Journey, as well as something connecting me to a spiritual tradition that seemed to answer some of my searching. From then on, I was off on my journey. I read many spiritual and self-help books and gradually set in place some basic spiritual practices for myself. I took an array of workshops, classes and retreats over a period of 4 to 5 years. The topics were varied, and I gleaned much of value from all these different books and teaching events, but nothing felt like the destination yet. I was still searching for several years, but I had caught a thread which would lead me to my answer. Each step along the way was a building block from which I learnt, grew and continued on. I was no longer lost in the wilderness, blindly looking around without a clear direction. Now, I was tracking my prey, following the scent of my calling and every step of the quest offered up gifts of insights, tests and learning along the way.

I did not forget the sense of remembrance of other times and places I experienced when reading "The Mists of Avalon". I increasingly had such experiences as I read other books, but also visiting different lands and historical places over the years in France, the UK, Eastern Europe and Spain. While I lived in London for a few years, I spent an enormous amount of time in the British Museum. I observed and intuitively felt into the eclectic range of archaeological artefacts from Ancient Egypt, Rome and Greece, Viking cultures and Iron Age Britain, medieval China and Japan, Native American, Mayan and other early South-American cultures. I sensed their history, their place of origin and somehow, on a level beyond my conscious mind, I remembered. I would be deeply moved, feeling many things without fully understanding why, experiencing almost like micro-downloads of Soul memories. The more I progressed along the road of my spiritual exploration, and the more I used my higher senses to interrogate the history around me, the more I "remembered" many of those times and places on a feeling level. The concept of past lives was not foreign. I had been raised outside of any orthodox religious structure by parents who believed in the afterlife and reincarnation. My mother's side of the family practiced routine tarot card readings and my parents took part in the odd spiritual séance. These are old traditions in France, where even some Presidents were known to consult their personal mediums for guidance. The "hocus-pocus" of it all was just a fact of life for me, so I never had to overcome ideological impediments in order to accept reincarnation as reality. I also never really thought about it. I knew we all had past lives which went back a very long way, and that was just that. Not a big deal. Often during history lessons at school, I would get a familiarity with some of the times and places we studied. The thought that I could have had another life in that era was on the back on my mind, but it never seemed like anything worth worrying about since there was no way of knowing for sure. I had my first clear yet brief flash of a past life memory when I was thirteen. I was sitting in my parents' car waiting for my mother to collect my grandmother from church choir practice. The window was open, letting in the subtle breeze of a balmy and peaceful spring day. All was calm and quiet, parked near the church. I felt so relaxed as I absent-mindedly gazed at the stone wall separating the church from the rest of the village. Within barely the fraction of a moment, I saw myself in an environment not too dissimilar to the scene I was looking upon: by a stone wall, close to a church, in some sort of monastery. In that twinkling of a moment, I had a host of feelings and awareness come up: the sense of being content in this monastery, the sense of being a man in that life, the enjoyment of working in the garden in the nice weather, the love of prayer and an overwhelming sense of peace and feeling in place. This all happened almost too fast to register, and yet was full, like the instant download of a time capsule. In the next moment, I was back in the back seat of my parents' car, with my window open, and I started crying. I cried not because I was sad, but simply because I was suddenly full of all these feelings from another time and place, and the memory moved me deeply. I had not known such peace in my short life, and part of me missed it. But it was not a big deal to me. I accepted this as simply something that was possibly the memory of another time and life. I did not really think about it much after that and just got on with my life.

The Case for Reincarnation

Reincarnation is a widely accepted concept in some religions and cultures around the world, like Buddhism, Hinduism, and the Sikh and Jainist traditions of India. Reincarnation featured in some old Celtic and Druidic traditions, and famous philosophers Plato and Pythagoras also considered it a fact of life. Yet, for many raised on a diet of Christianity, Islam or Judaism, accepting the existence of reincarnation can be a stretch. These faiths favour of the idea of us having one life and then dying to spend the rest of eternity in an unchanging afterlife realm, in some version of either heaven or hell. The main argument for the theory of having only one life is that there is no proof in favour of reincarnation. My answer is: where is the proof of a constant afterlife heaven or hell? Even if I set aside my own memories of other times and incarnations, I feel there is much more proof of reincarnation than there is of the one-life paradigm. Even within the framework of a Christian, or

Christian-adjacent belief, the concept of having only one life makes little sense. Isn't God supposed to be all loving? Does Christianity not teach the importance of developing god-like qualities such as acceptance, unconditional love, kindness and forgiveness? Yet, you would in the same breath have us believe that such a kind, forgiving and loving God would give his children souls only one chance to get it right, or otherwise rot in a horror-story hell of cruel, gruesome torture for all eternity??? How is that not a complete irreconcilable inconsistency? I am sorry but the "God works in mysterious ways" axiom does not explain this conflict in dogma. If God was indeed the kind, loving, compassionate, patient, and forgiving All-Father that He is, he would, like any good parent, guide and support his children to continue their learning, face their lessons and grow from them until they became more like Him. No loving and forgiving parents would condemn their children to eternal torture after only one chance to get it right!

There are other forms of evidence in favour reincarnation. If you look around online but possibly even in your own wider entourage, you may find examples of kids who come apparently already loaded up with particular gifts, abilities or memories that we cannot simply explain as imagination or good luck. I once had among my acquaintances a young boy who could speak and understand some French in his early years, even though he had been born in an English-speaking country, of English-speaking parents, and was never taught French by anyone. Once he became a little older however, the spiritual amnesia set in and he lost this ability. Some kids are born with amazing capabilities at things like playing an instrument. And I am sorry, but even with some lessons, there is no way that a three-year-old can play the piano, the guitar or the drum like an experienced musician unless they have done it before, and brought this skill with them into their new incarnation. Think about it rationally: what makes more sense? That a child should have just an instant, incredible ability and level of skill coming out of nowhere? Or that they, as a soul, were in their last life an amazing musician, who worked to develop these skills for a long time, brought some of this along with them, and are now simply continuing on from where they left off? Of course, this means training and wiring a new little child body to do what they know, as a soul, how to do, but it explains the amazing natural talent and instinct that such little souls have. I have also watched and read many stories of children having clear, sometimes proven accurate, memories of their previous lives, and even memories of the 'waiting' on the inner planes before reincarnating. Some of those stories out there are probably hoaxes, but some appear genuine. My own experience of a past-life memory, unexpected and unbidden, at age 13 is another example. I also remember, in my teens, having a strange dream of seeing a little boy I knew who had died in sudden and tragic circumstances a few years prior. In my dream, I saw this little soul in a place which looked like a strange dimension of a train-station. Within this place was reconstructed the home and local street that this boy had been living in before he died. Supportive spirits surrounded him and cared for him while they waiting for his "train". The little boy was in transit, kept in a safe and familiar place, while he waited for his train back to where he had accidentally left too early from. This was a very clear feeling and one that left me a bit confused and stirred up when I woke up. Not long after I had this dream, we learnt his parents were having another baby boy. When the little boy was born, and grew, he was enormously like their first son who had died. He looked enormously similar, and had a similar temperament and look in his eyes. Was this just a dream?

A coincidence? Or was that soul indeed waiting to come back and have another go at the life that was cut too short because of an unexpected accident?

Some of you may then say: "Oh, but what about the people who have a near-death experience, and see a tunnel and beings of light or dead loved ones welcoming them?" My answer is: What does this actually prove? It simply proves that when we die, the soul undergoes a transition into a different dimension and reality, where perhaps we reside for a time…. but not necessarily forever! Reincarnation does not mean that we automatically die in one body and reincarnate instantly into a new body. From what I have learnt along the way, such lateral soul transfers can occur but they are extremely rare and happen only in specific cases. For everyone else, the recently passed soul undergoes an in-depth process of review, learning and integration of their life, which unfolds on the inner planes of existence. This is a process called Bardo, which the teachings of the Buddhism refer to. As one person dies, their soul can go through the 'tunnel of light' and even meet the souls of some of their dead loved ones to welcome them with a familiar face as they prepare for the afterlife review work which will both complete their recently finished life, and prepare them for the next. This Bardo process, in itself, makes so much more sense that the idea of one life and then you're done, because this is how life works, and this is how nature works and this is how evolution works. We have experiences, we have the opportunity to review and learn from them, and then we have another go. Why would death be any different?

Let us remind ourselves of the ancient wisdom of "As above, so below", and its fractal repetition of the same pattern and processes at different levels of Creation. As such, what we observe within us and around us in the natural world is a lower correspondence reflection of how things work on more expansive levels. Nature lives in cycles. We have the cycles of our days and nights, defined by the rotation of our Earth upon its axis, while the sun's light shines on one side of it. We have the solar year and the cycle of the seasons, defined by the elliptical rotation of our Earth around the Sun. We have a moon cycle, as the moon circles around our planet, which also affects the ocean tides and many other things such as plant growth, hair growth and animal behaviour. We have women's reproductive cycles, also linked to the magnetism of the moon cycles as well as a woman's own life cycles and emotions. We have a cycle for the precession of the equinoxes, defined by the wobbling of our planet's central axis over a cycle of about 25,800 years. This cycle gives us the periods of time we call astrological ages, which influence and define the spiritual ideals and lessons that our planet must integrate to embrace its evolution. Have you heard about the Age of Aquarius? This refers to the new astrological age we are currently entering, as defined by the constellation that the sun rises in for this phase of the cycle. We also have the Milankovitch cycles, defined by the combination of the angle and direction of our planet's axis and the variations in the elongation of the ellipse that our planet follows around the sun. The Milankovitch cycle causes periodical ice ages and changes in climate. As you can see, we literally exist within an ever-expanding dance of repeating cycles! Suns and planets have life cycles, so do stars, and plants and animals… and so do we. The very cells in our bodies have life cycles, with cells in certain organs living longer than others, and brand new cells replacing those who have died, only for the cycle to repeat. Even our sleep has cycles and circadian rhythms! Everything changes all the time; everything cycles round and round; everything that goes around comes back around. Plants grow and flower in springs, produce fruits and seeds in summer, wither and drop in autumn, then lie in rest and regeneration in winter, only to begin the cycle again in the next year! Trees produce new leaves and new growth in spring, grow stronger and larger branches, and sometimes fruit, throughout springs and summer. In autumn, trees withdraw a degree of their life force and sap into themselves just as the Soul Tree withdraws the energy of its Soul back up into the higher planes after death. The Tree's energy is allowed to integrate, rest and rejuvenate within their roots during winter, just as the Soul does in the period between embodiments. New seeds are dropped onto the ground gestate within the womb of the earth to prepare for new growth in spring. These are the cycles of life, and they are everywhere. What makes us think that our life and death would be any different?

Any student of history will notice similar cycles at play. Nations and empires rise, expand, degrade and fall according to recognisable stages. This cycle repeats throughout history, dressed up differently but the same in essence. The evolution of ideas, ideologies and scientific paradigms also runs in cycles. Thomas Khun's work on the shifting in scientific paradigms exposes this rhythm to the evolution of scientific knowledge and accepted scientific paradigms. Religions and their beliefs rise and fall in the same manner. Our physical lives are no exceptions. We are born, we grow up, we get old and we die. Everyone follows the same cycle. Our relationships, projects, jobs and phases of subjective experience follows cycles too: beginnings and new creations, expansion and exploration, winding down and wrapping up, ending and letting go, to then begin again with something new.

Although the cycles repeat, again and again, there is an overarching sense of progression and forward movement. Each cycle builds on the one before in order to generate progress and growth. A tree will shed its leaves and withdraw its life force every winter, but it does not start from scratch again in spring; it continues to build upon the growth of the previous year. We may end one relationship and then start a new one, but the new relationship is based on the experience and learning of the previous relationship. What we learnt from the previous cycle will, hopefully, help us do better in the next one. So what we have is cyclic repetition (a circle) within a larger pattern of forward progress (a upward line). Combine the circle pattern of cycles and the linear pattern of ongoing progress and what you get is a spiral…. like our DNA, like the ancient spiral symbol which held so much meaning to ancient cultures. Darwinian thought speaks of this progressive evolution over time: those who survive are those who adapt to cyclically changing circumstances. Plants have evolved, animals have evolved and humans have evolved. Those who did not go with the memo of constant natural change, and adapt to it, did not survive.

Once we discern this spiral pattern of cyclic existence within an overarching upward evolution, it becomes ridiculous to assume that this amazing divine design applies to every single thing in Creation -from the life cycle of a cell to that of a Universe-but does not apply to the life of Souls. Why would our Soul go through one cycle of incarnation and learning, to then sit in some eternal, stagnant state of heavenly or hellish suspension, forever unchanging? Why would these precious vehicle of experience no longer flow with life's cycles and evolve? Once we widen our minds to perceive the cycles, rhythms and movements of Creation, reincarnation becomes the only reality which matches the way everything works.

Trees grow by cyclically sprouting new leaves and growing new branches. Eventually, the Tree drop old leaves and dead branches. Our Soul Tree (our Oversouls or Higher Selves) are no different: they grow leaves, which are the embodiment of the Souls. Souls are the little branches hanging off the even bigger branches of our Soul Groups. Eventually, the little leaf embodiments die and fall; this is us, as fragile, short-lived body minds. But the branch is still alive and grows new leaves on the same branch in the next spring of life. This is reincarnation: like leaves, our body-minds end and drop off the branch, but the Soul endures to extend its energy to grow new leaves, new life, and new soul extensions.

The Soul Tree and Reincarnation

As above, so below. The pattern of spiritual reincarnation is reflected in the cycles ever-present in nature. At a more expansive level, Unified Source which imploded, exploded and sprung forth into Life is like the giant cosmic seed of All That Is: filled with potential life force and energy, erupting and shooting into many seedlings and lifeforms. Some of these seedlings became universes, or galaxies, some became Monads, which divided into Soul Trees. One of those trees is the one who are a part of.

You, as the human person that you are -with a face, name, address and favourite food-are only one leaf on your Soul Tree. Like any leaf on a deciduous tree, you will, at the end of this leaf life-cycle, wither, die and fall. The life force which was sustaining your body-mind will withdraw back into the branch, and into the tree, just like real trees do by withdrawing their life force into their core and roots in winter. Does a leaf on a tree reincarnate in the next spring? No. That leaf is dead and gone forever. However, the tree is still alive, and so is the branch. The Soul energy which was withdrawn from the dying leaves endures, and uploads the learning gained during its recent embodiment. Part of this process of integration in-between embodiments is the Bardo process, which we explore in the next section. The Soul's energy can, at any time, project its energy into matter again to create new embodiments, like the branch can grow new leaves. The new leaves that grow in spring are not the same leaves which were there the previous year. Yet they come from the same tree, and the same branch, and will be energised with the same life force and tree wisdom which imbued the previous year's leaves

So it is with the Soul Tree. Each personality embodiment is but one leaf on a tree. When this embodiment dies, it simply dies. It is not the body-mind, or even your constructed sense of personality, which endures beyond death and into reincarnation. Only the twig, the branch and tree endure into the reincarnational cycles. The soul endures, the Oversoul endures, the Monad endures, but the embodiment well and truly falls off the tree at the end of this incarnation. It is not you as the personality who reincarnates, it is you as the Soul, and beyond as Spirit. This is an enormously important fact to understand because there is, from my experience, much glamour and mistaken self-reference among those in the new age movement, when speaking of their 'past lives'.

If you truly understand that the body-mind personality does not reincarnate, then you logically understand that the *you* that is the ego-personality cannot have past lives, or future lives. The only life you -as an ego-personality - have ever had is who you are now. All you have ever been as a personality is who you are now. All your conscious mind knows is what you have experienced in this life. For anyone who is still in a state of personality identification to say "I was so and so in a past life" is a complete misnomer, because the little I never existed before this life. A leaf on a tree never was another leaf.

Only the disciple who has completed Soul Merge in an integrated way, and who is genuinely identified at a minimum at Soul level, can speak of having past lives.

Many ego-identified individuals seek knowledge of past lives for all the wrong reasons: wanting to be someone else and escape who they are now, wanting to have been someone important, wanting to feel special, wanting to impress others, wanting more stories to feed into their personal myth… all of which denotes poor self-esteem, a lack of self-love and an unhealthy need for recognition. A true initiate remembers past lives as part of the process of piecing together the steps of their evolutionary lessons through time. Feelings and memories from other lives will also present as part of the process of soul braiding described in the previous chapter. This is part of clearing our Soul karma, by confronting and processing the unresolved energy and disharmony from other embodiments on the same branch as us. Once this unresolved karmic energy from other leaves is purified and harmonised, it feeds into the soul's evolution and raising of vibration. These initiates may tell some people who are close to them about previous Soul embodiments, but they rarely make grand public claims about who "they" were. They are too busy working on their growth, clearing vast amounts of energy and serving selflessly to be going around the world blowing their own trumpets. Any claim made on their part is about serving and furthering the work of spiritual service, not about making themselves look important or special. Remembering past lives is only useful if it helps you heal, integrate the necessary lessons and become a more evolved and masterful version of yourself now. If past lives are used to feel special, impress others or escape from a life you judge, then it is all about ego, not about truth.

The levels of Soul - the Buddhic vehicle–and any of the higher bodies you may have activated on the higher mental plane and beyond, endure in the same way that the branches of a tree endure through the winter and into the next spring. Each new embodiment is created as a co-creation between Soul and Gaia. As creatures, we are absolutely a part of the Earth. Individual Soul interfaces with the Soul aspect of Mother Earth through the level called Primal Soul. This is like the lowest level of the Buddhic plane and the lowest level of our Soul, through which we interface with the lower mental, astral and physical realms. Primal Soul is also where the imprints of karma from previous lives on this planet is stored. When our Soul branch grows new leaves, imprints from Primal Soul level can be downloaded into the lower bodies and into our karmic blueprint for that embodiment. This is how the Soul Tree seeks to ensure that we continue with our Soul learning by experiencing the consequences of previous life choices, giving us a chance to harmonise past karma. Our lower bodies are made of the mental, astral and physical matter from Mother Earth, who provides what Soul needs to build a vehicle; this includes the genetic material from our parents, which is also made of matter from Mother Earth. The body-mind is then en-souled and animated by the life of the Soul. Soul is in turn animated by the life of its branch, which is turn is animated by the Soul Tree. At the time of death, the life which animated the embodiment for its entire lifespan withdraws back into the branch. As this en-souling energy withdraws from the lower bodies, it takes with it the integrated wisdom, learning and unresolved issues from that embodiment, to be miniaturised and stored at Primal Soul level in readiness for download into the next relevant embodiment. This is how evolution continues from life to life: while the lower bodies cease to exist, the actualised learning, wisdom and the issues left unresolved are uploaded to the Soul, like you would save a file on your computer. This saved Knowing and karma will then be used to inform the next relevant leaf on the branch: this is what we call reincarnation, when a new embodiment is informed by the Knowing and experience of a previous leaf. The wisdom, lessons and issues from a previous life are saved and then used to form the basis of the next evolutionary steps of the Soul, in another embodied expression. In order to integrate its learning from each incarnation and progress into the next, Soul undergoes a process of review and learning after death, which is the Bardo process. If you ever wondered why people who have near-death experiences have their lives quickly flashing before their eyes, this is why. This phenomenon is a first quick wrap up and backup of the life's experiences and lessons in preparation for Bardo.

The Bardo Process

When an embodiment dies, The Soul withdraws and disconnects from the physical-etheric body after it has expired, a process which takes about three days and is why most ancient funerary practices recommend a period of at least three days allowed for preparation of the body and a wake before burial or cremation. This gives the soul time to sever the silver cord and dissolve the fine etheric connections which have, for the person's lifetime, connected the physical body to the other more refined bodies. After this initial dissolving begins a period of progressive withdrawal to other lower planes of existence, reviewing and gradually relinquishing and returning to Mother Earth the energetic matter of the lower bodies.

Once the Soul energy has disconnected from the physical body and dissolved the etheric body, it withdraws for a time onto the astral plane in order to review and upload emotional lessons, and dissolve the astral body. Some Souls get stuck on the astral plane for a longer time if they cling to and over-identify with their emotional attachments and issues from the life, unable to move on into the next phase of their passing. Loved ones who were left behind in the world of the living can also make the departed soul's transition through the astral plane more difficult if they emotionally hold on, refusing to allow them to continue on their eternal journey. Souls who get stuck on the astral plane can easily lose track of time, going round in circles with their unfinished emotional issues and attachments, reliving imagined scenarios of what they cannot let go of. These astral entities are the ghosts that many mediums contact, and there is very little enlightenment to be gained from communicating with them.

Next is the withdrawal to the lower mental plane, and this is where many people who identified as their body-mind stop and undergo the main work of their Bardo review process before dissolving the lower mental body and withdrawing their energy to Primal Soul level, which is the lowest part of the Buddhic vehicle, and where karmic imprints are stored. Every time a Soul withdraws from and dissolves their bodies on the three lower planes, they also dissolve the memories stored in the physical-etheric, astral and lower mental bodies. This is why we forget most of what happened in previous lives. The only things we remember is what was stored and integrated at Soul level. This is also why more evolved Souls, who have lived after completing Soul Merge and beyond, can have some past lives memories: the Soul was actually embodied and grounded, having first-hand experiences. Any memory stored within the lower bodies is still dissolved upon death, however. Only Soul memories endure.

Souls who have advanced further on the path of initiation and activated the Buddhic body and beyond continue their withdrawal of their consciousness and energy to yet higher planes. Each Soul will withdraw to its highest attained-to plane and dimension of existence to complete their Bardo. This means that more evolved

Souls benefit from the more expansive perspective of the higher planes as they undergo Bardo.

The Bardo process is the review and integration which occurs after the termination of a particular embodiment in order to consolidate the Soul's learning before the next incarnational experience. Remember that the purpose of our living is to experience, explore, learn and evolve so we can contribute our bits of acquired wisdom towards the greater learning of our Source. The individual leaf-embodiment gathers learning, then bring this learning back to their branch. The branch uploads the learning back to the Soul Tree, who brings the learning back to the Monadic Forest and so on, eventually all the way back to Source. Both the process of living and the process of dying feed into the process of spiritual evolution.

Our embodied incarnations play a dual role in their evolutionary contributions, since they are a bridge between Soul and Earth. Earth incarnations are part of our spiritual schooling as individual Souls, but also contribute to the collective spiritual evolution of humanity, which is a part of planet Earth. Every evolutionary lesson we integrate and express contributes to the evolution of Soul, and to the evolution of humanity and the planet. Everything in our existence is about being part of, and contributing to, something greater. Most people forget this. Earth life is not just about chasing our personal happiness and satisfying urges and pleasures, nor is it about enduring it like a meaningless ordeal until we escape into a heavenly realm. Life is a school and an opportunity to contribute to our evolution as well as the planet's. When approached as such, one can orient their consciousness to use every experience which presents as an opportunity to learn something, to develop desirable qualities, to grow, and even as an opportunity to be of service. When you adopt this approach, every encounter is meaningful, every challenge carries within it the seed of a gift and everything has purpose. This utilitarian attitude enables our life to foster value for ourselves and for the world. We become a better person through the embracing and appreciating of what life throws at us.

Yet, how often do we see people complaining about their lot? Wanting life to always be easy? Expecting they should have the right to get anything they want, whenever they want? Wanting life to be free of pain? Free of uncertainty? What growth is there in an existence where we are never challenged? How can we expand our experience if we never have to step into the unknown? Never have to work hard at anything? How can we gain compassion for the suffering of others if our heart is never broken? What kind of courage can we develop from living in constant comfort and certainty? What kind of wisdom can be gained from being coddled? Our bodies grow unfit and weak if we never overcome our laziness in order to exercise. Our immune system grows inefficient if we are never exposed to pathogens. This is how life works on this planet: We meet resistance, we meet challenges, we are stretched past our comfort zones, we are asked to grow beyond our current level of competence, and this is how we widen our evolutionary horizons. The correct life attitude means welcoming what life throws at us and doing our best to turn it into something valuable. It's not about perfection; it's about having a go and doing our best. This is how we improve and grow. Spiritual evolution requires more than book-learning or an intellectual understanding of the lessons. Soul needs to have experiences. We must participate in the process of lie, and allow ourselves to be changed by our experiences in a way which is about love, wisdom and truth. Theoretical learning does not count in the Soul's evolution. We must be transformed by and embody the essence of the lessons we've learnt. This is the learning we get to take to the Soul, as we depart this Earth.

Part of how the Soul integrates the learning of each embodiment is through the Bardo process. After death and generally for about a third of the duration of the life which has just ended, the soul undertakes a sort of dream-like review of that life: What actually happened, how we felt, how we made others feel and the effect we had on people and the world around us. This is our karma. Through our choices, thoughts, behaviours and actions, we impact and effect our self, others and the world around us. Facing our karma, learning from it and finding a way to accept and rebalance it is a key part of evolution. The Bardo review process is designed to support and give an extra chance to the recently passed Soul to integrate their life's lessons. Many people go through life without thorough reflection on their deeds, their feelings, their influence or the effect they have on other people through both their actions and the use of their energy. Everything we do, everything we think, everything we say and every way we throw our energy around has an effect. All our choices, on every level, have consequences. Many people have an amount of avoidance and denial, particularly in relations to uncomfortable realities and painful feelings. People take refuge in a sense of being 'right' instead of questioning themselves to find deeper truth. People can live through their imagination, colouring their reality in order to make it more palatable to their fear-based, selfish ego. To the ego-identified person, being wrong is humiliating, losing control is scary, and not getting what we want hurts. It is easier to avoid and deny the unpleasantness of it all and lie to ourselves to make life seemingly easier. But when we lie to ourselves, our lives become a lie. Often, we forget where the lies began and much of our avoidance and denial become unconscious.

After we die, the Bardo review offers us the opportunity to face our life, our deeds, our actual feelings and our impact on others without the veils of avoidance and denial. It is an act of unpeeling the layers of subjective untruth we covered our experience with and face the reality of our choices and feelings. It is up to each of us to choose whether we embrace the process gracefully, or whether we resist and struggle to accept our lessons. Even at that point after death, the individual Soul still has free will about whether we partner with the Universe as She tries to teach us our lessons, or whether we cling to our illusions, coping strategies, and narratives. The Bardo review completes the process of our last incarnation and prepares us for the next one, by consolidating the Knowing which will inform the next leaf in the journey.

Once the Bardo process is complete, the soul enters a period of waiting to incarnate again. How long this wait is varies, depending on factors like the level of evolution of the Soul, the availability of appropriate embodiments for that Soul to continue its evolution, and the potential call to spiritual service.

When we are finally assigned an embodiment, Soul begins the process of connecting with the potential parents, and precipitating another set of lower bodies in co-creation with the parental genetic lineages and Mother Earth, who lends us the matter to build our bodies. Contrary to popular new-age folklore, few Souls get to choose their parents like we would when shopping for a nice suit. Like most things in life, which family we are born into is a matter of physics; more specifically magnetic attraction. A Soul is drawn towards particular parents, family, place and general environment for reasons like unresolved karma, old Soul attachments, strong bonds of love or strong bonds of enmity through time, a call to a service mission or the need for specific lessons and experiences provided by that environment. We may barely gain insight into the humbling perfection with which the Universe orchestrates circumstances and experiences for evolving souls. Those who evolve to a point of recalling some of their Soul's journey will in moments receive inklings of this perfect design, yet not be able to fully grasp it. This same perfection will be present in the manifestation of the circumstances of your birth and key encounters in early life. No one is born in their family by mistake, and nothing happens at random. As we grow older, we have more scope for the use or abuse of our free will, and can decide to follow Spirit's design or ignore it. Yet, everything that was a major part of our birth and growing up experience will, in some form or another, serve our learning, evolution and the harmonising of past karma.

What is karma exactly? Simply put: the consequences of our choices over time. Every choice we make sets in motions particular responses and energy. If we make choices of love, we accrue our karma of love. If we make choices of fear, we accrue our karma of fear. The Universe will guide us through the learning and experiences we need to make better choices. Better choices in the eyes of Spirit are choices which are more in harmony with the nature of our Universe, or in other words: choices of higher love, wisdom and enlightenment. Therefore, if we carelessly cause great harm, we may have to experience similar harm ourselves in order to learn empathy, compassion and realise that we do not want to inflict that kind of harm on others anymore. If we effect great love and evolutionary benefits, we will more gracefully flow forward on our evolutionary journey towards the realisation of our Divine potential. This is, again, like physics. It is not personal; it is simply how the great Universal Machine works in order to support the learning, evolution and return home of all of Its moving parts.

In every incarnation, we are born into a life context which will set us up for the set of experiences and learning we need. It is then up to us to choose, in each and every moment, to either welcome our experiences as feedback to evolve into a better version of ourselves, or to complain, rage, resist or feel sorry for ourselves. We are an important component which defines how our lives are manifested. How we handle our lessons goes a long way towards creating our future, but that's not all. We have a say, and how we use our free will to choose what we choose is a key input in the equation. The Universe, in Her infinite benevolence, does not simply impose upon us apparently random experiences to serve our evolution. In order to teach us to make wiser choices, She always takes our input into account. Manifestation is, to varying degrees, a process of co-creation between us and the Universe. Our intelligent Universe computes our choices and intentions with our evolutionary needs, and the needs of the Whole. She then feeds the results of this co-creation back to us in a way that is geared towards helping us learn to make wiser, move loving and spiritually intelligent choices. In order for us to learn, we must experience the consequences of our choices. If we make a choice and experience our life going to shit because of it, we hopefully will realise that we made a bad choice and learn a valuable lesson from it. Learning from the consequences of our choices requires that we self-reflect enough to monitor the results of our actions, and that we take responsibility for our choices and their manifest consequences. God and Goddess are patient parents existing within a timeless reality, but it does not mean They are permissive parents. Most Souls will get away for a time with making selfish, fear-based choices without confronting immediate unpleasant consequences. But, sooner or later, whether in this life or the next, everyone gets their just deserts as their karma catches up with them. This is not a case of "vengeful God", but one of Universal benevolent guidance. To project nasty little human traits like vengefulness upon the Divine is ridiculous and small-minded. Karma is not revenge, it is our creation coming back to us. Karma is our responsibility. The consequences of our choices return to us to show us what we created, and teach us what we most need to learn. Unresolved karma is the energy of lessons still incomplete or unlearnt. This energy returns to us to be harmonised, turned into love and realigned within the Universal Order. Using a modern metaphor, one could say that life is a bit like a giant multi-dimensional computer. We are the users and Universal Intelligence in its various forms is the software. We input information into the system through our thoughts, emotional expressions, choices, behaviour, energetic outputs and actions. These inputs set energy in motion and co-creates with the Great Universal Software. The Universe uses our input, processes it through its "nurture of evolution" software and generates the experiences we need. We get the consequences of the choices we made, with just a little dose of spiritual mirroring to help us learn to make ever better choices. We always get what we put out for, even though it may not manifest the way our ego intended. We will get what we, as Souls, need. The ability to receive Life's gifts of Universal mirroring with gratitude and humility is a key factor in the Soul's ability to evolve.

While every embodiment exists to fulfil the primary Universal directive to experience, learn and evolve, each embodiment has its own purpose. Some embodiments exist only to have a new set of targeted experience which the Soul Tree has not had before, or wants to learn more about. Some embodiments' are about clearing karma which is impeding their Soul lineage from progressing into the next phase of its evolution; we call these clean-up embodiments. Some embodiments are aimed at developing particular skills and abilities. Some embodiments are strongly focused on service and giving back. Some embodiments combine elements of all the above, as the Soul seeks to integrate and consolidate its learning into one expression. Not every Soul is at the same level of evolution, but every Soul extension embodiment has a life purpose. Each leaf must follow, with a degree of free will, the directives of the Soul Tree. Every leaf must, to whatever small or large degree, contribute something of value to the evolution of the entire Soul Tree. This is the purpose of this whole amazing journey after all! To refuse to do this, using our free will to go against what is for the higher good of our spiritual Tree family, will eventually bear consequences. Leaves which are an impediment to the spiritual progression of their branch, or who bring spiritual illness to their Soul Tree, will compassionately be allowed to dry on the branch and fall. This is a confronting reality for our small egos who like to believe that we have absolute right of control over our existence. We are not sacred cows and the Universe does not revolve around us. Each and every one of us, as individual embodiments of our Soul Tree's energy, are here to serve the Tree and play our part in the Universal dance of evolution. The Higher Self who sustains us and guides is the boss; not the other way around. It may sound drab to the self-absorbed ego, but allowing ourselves to get sucked into place in this great evolutionary dance feels better than anything else. We will never feel as in place and content as when we answer the call to our spiritual destiny, and partner with our Soul Tree.

Reincarnation and Time

Each embodiment, or soul extension, is but one stream of the Soul's energy extending into matter. Each Soul has many such soul extensions through space and time, in the past, the future, and the present, on this planet and others. As human beings, we experience our lives clothed in physical matter and qualified by the five physical senses. This allows us to move and act within the concreteness of the third dimension and to experience time as linear. The Soul, however, experiences time through the fourth dimensional consciousness of flow. More expansive levels of our Soul-Tree experience time as a unity (fifth dimensional consciousness), an is-ness (sixth dimensional consciousness), and beyond into multidimensional realities the monkey-mind cannot grasp. This means that as far as the Soul is concerned, the experience of time and of reincarnation is a tangible sense of interconnected flowing from one moment and one life into the next. The connections between moments, between choices and their consequences are felt tangibly as they flow into one another, feed into one another, and cause one another. This linear chain of cause and consequence allows the Soul to learn: if I do this, then this happens, if I choose this, then this is the consequence. Yet this does not mean that the wheel of reincarnation always turns in a chronological manner within linear time. The time experience of the Higher Self, or Oversoul, is more like a unified ocean or a matrix.

The experience of time is a function of movement in space, and particularly the motion of consciousness through space. We will explore this topic further in the next chapter. My point here is that a Soul Tree may choose, through its branches and Souls, to project soul extensions anywhere in space and time. This would be a little like diving into a space-time pool: You can choose to dive anywhere into that pool, and therefore manifest leaf-embodiments at any place in space or any point in time, without the need to follow a particular linear order. Given that the Buddhic vehicle's experience is fourth-dimensional, our subjective journey of learning will still follow a linear flow and progression, regardless of where or when we incarnate… But the context of our next life experience could be anywhere or anytime. Our next leaf may be in the past, but our Soul learning will continue on from where we left off in this life. For the most part however, Souls journey through eternity in more or less a chronological order, because this tends to be easier for the Soul. After all, imagine the shock and difficulty of adaptation for a Soul living life after life in the 10th century, then the 11th century…. Then suddenly jumping to a life in the 21st century. The changes in technology themselves could overwhelm the Soul's capacity to adapt, and that's not even going into the drastic cultural and ideological changes made in the space of nine centuries! However, it does occasionally happen that Souls have incarnation out of time. You last life may have been a century ago, or it may have been fifty years into the future. I know this sound nonsensical to the rational mind and its third-dimensional mode of functioning, but it does happen more than most people realise!

Parallel Embodiments and Ascension Vehicles

And there's more! Oversouls and Souls will usually project several soul extension embodiments in rounds, or cycles of incarnations which can land into any time or space, and also within the same time-space. Yes, this means that right now there are other versions of us, other versions of our Soul energy, walking about in the world in this very time! Some will be younger than you, some older and some close to your age. Some might even overlap with your lifetime only by a handful of years. Some will be men, some will be women, and they will exist all over the world having an array of different lives and experiences. Most are unlikely to ever meet another version of themselves however, as the Soul Tree tends to keep them away from each other so their experience and learning is different and varied. Only in very rare cases, and for specific reasons, do we see more than one version of the same Soul Tree energy in the same time *and* space. Even then, these two individuals may not even notice each other, or they may in some cases feel magnetically repelled.

The reality of parallel embodiments is, in my experience, one that often gets the most hostile reactions from spiritual students. The ego, after all, wants to be the favourite and likes to think of itself as special. The idea of not being the only "me" is experienced as a threat to our egoic sense of importance. It can also be felt as competition, like jealous siblings fighting to be the favourite. These reactions are a sign that the student is still, to a large degree, identified with the separate egoic self. The Soul and the Higher Self simply experience these multiple soul extensions as "myself", and certainly nothing to feel threatened by. Remember that the Monad, Oversoul and the Soul are following our primary Creational directive: to go forth, have experiences, learn and evolve. If you were trying to be efficient in this process, wouldn't you put as many pots on the stove as you could at the same time? From an operational point of view, it makes absolute sense to multitask. It is only our fat little egos who don't like to be reminded of how small we are in the greater scheme of things. Parallel embodiments are like a team of busy incarnational bees, working on various life purposes, all of which are relevant to have in this space-time. Parallel embodiment can also be backups, in case other embodiments come to an unscheduled end or don't fulfil their assigned function and purpose. There are consequences to our choice to either bring value or not bring value to our Soul Tree. Leaves who, over time, keep making choices which are destructive to the health of the Tree will need to be terminated in order to preserve the health and evolution of the Soul Tree.

Each Soul extension will hopefully serve the evolutionary progress of their Soul Tree. When a Soul leaf embodiment does well in bringing value to their Tree, the Soul Tree will regard them as a good idea: interesting and precious. Each branch will have a leaf which outperforms the others in bringing evolutionary value to the Tree. This leaf will be chosen as the ascension vehicle for the entire branch. The ascension vehicle will be the Soul extension tasked with integrating the Knowing and energy of other leaves in order to boost the Tree's evolution, bandwidth and learning. The same applies at the next level, where each Oversoul will have some branches performing better than others, and therefore assign more attention and support to those best serving the Soul Tree's evolution. This is a matter of betting on the winning horse. If a leaf is doing well at serving the purpose and evolution of the Soul Tree, then it is rewarded with more resources, in the form of more energy and access to more of the Tree's Knowing. As far as the Soul Tree is concerned, it's an investment. This is, again, thoroughly efficient and will make sense to anyone who has managed the logistics of any business, project or army: resources are allocated where they will bring the best result on investment. The Universe is, if nothing, an efficient merit-based system. If you put in the work and achieve the results, you will receive more energy and support; if you prove more of a liability in evolutionary terms, then you may end up being find your spiritual resources diminished and reassigned to the other more useful leaves on your branch. How can you ensure you become the ascension vehicle on your branch? Be a good idea to your Soul Tree!

The Soul evolves and progresses through spiritual initiation. Eventually, the Soul begins the process of Soul and Monadic braiding, whereby they integrate, purify and expand into the energy, learning and karma of other aspects of their Soul branch and Soul Tree. This begins with the integration and clearing of the energy of past leaves closest on the same little Soul branch. As the Soul progresses it gradually expands out to other branches, then to more of the Soul Tree, and beyond into the Monad. The more the Soul grows and expands its bandwidth through the process of initiation, the more Knowing and energy it integrates on a wider level of the Monad. The process of Soul Braiding and Monadic braiding also includes the integration of parallel embodiments. Remember that as far as the Higher Self is concerned, our supposed "past lives" embodiments exist within a unity of time, as if at the same time. This ascension vehicle will be the expression through which the Soul Tree consolidates its energy. The more the initiate progresses through the higher initiations, the more of the Soul Tree's energy is integrated into them, and the fewer other parallel versions of them we find in the same time and space. This is because the energy of the Soul Tree focuses more through the main ascension vehicle.

That some students feel threatened in the spiritual sense by the existence of parallel embodiment stems, in parts, from this intuitive knowing that, should they not perform in evolutionary terms, or should they become a long-term liability to the tree, they may end up seeing their energy absorbed into another version of themselves. It is, of course, only the separate little personality ego which fears such things. The soul knows and feels all its embodiments to be simply another finger on its own hand, simply other aspects of itself. The soul celebrates the advent of an ascension vehicle when one of its leaf children is doing well. The Soul Tree, and all the master branches on the Tree, cheer on and champion this winning leaf by investing in its continued success. The fear-based ego exists in competitive scarcity consciousness, Soul and Spirit know that every win that a leaf makes is a win for the entire tree. The Soul Tree does not compete with itself, it works as a team and is unattached.

Cycles of Incarnations and Major Incarnations

Like everything else, the Soul's eternal journey through time and space on this planet works in cycles. Each incarnation is a cycle, but the Soul also projects its energy into matter in rounds, or cycles of 12 major incarnations. Each of these incarnation cycles is like a round of learning for the Soul. The first major incarnation is the beginning of a new phase of learning, and the twelfth incarnation in the cycle forms the completion and culmination of that cycle of evolutionary learning. These 12 major incarnations can also be interspersed with minor and major-minor incarnations.

A major incarnation is one where the Soul undergoes crucial learning and evolutionary progression, and potentially service work. Major incarnations are where the Soul really moves forward in the initiation process, undergoes tangible growth and possibly undertakes major service projects. In support of the achievements of major incarnation, major-minor incarnation are usually about processing and clearing karma in order to remove karmic impediments to the Soul's progression. Minor embodiments are more limited in scope, and can easily be created through nothing more than the Soul's curiosity or attachments. Minor embodiments are about having particular experiences, perhaps living out one's exploration of an area of interest, or trying to live one's fairy-tale, or even simply answering a persistent question. Some of these minor incarnations may be necessary as part of the Soul's exploration of various topics and experiences, in order to round out its learning. Yet it can be very easy for the undisciplined Soul to create unnecessary minor incarnations simply by clinging to unrequited fantasies, holding on to grudges or wishing you could be someone else. The more energy the Soul has, the easier it is to manifest and extend new, unnecessary incarnations. Do you secretly dream of being a famous chef but know it is not your path of highest calling? You may just end up creating a soul extension where this happens. This may seem relatively harmless, but it all depends on how that chef incarnation goes. What if that embodiment misbehaves and creates extra binding karma for the Soul to clear? That ends up just being more trouble than it's worth, delaying the Soul's evolution rather than helping it along. In the end, creating anything unnecessary in our evolution is not clever, it's a risk. It is better to stick to our path and calling, and let go of everything which no longer serves our higher calling.

****

Every incarnation is simply one leaf on the tree, yet each of them has a purpose and function. Each incarnation is but one day in the life of the Soul, and each incarnational cycle is but one step in the Soul's eternal journey of learning. To remember this simple fact of life puts many things into perspective. Many of the small things that our fearful ego obsesses about actually don't really matter most of the time. If you can get your ego out of the way, the reality of our being a small part of a much larger being is in truth deeply comforting. It means we are never alone. It means we are always connected to something larger than ourselves, and always guided by it, if we will only listen and partner with it. It means our little lives can contribute, to any small or larger degree, to the evolution of a part of Creation. We have purpose. We are meaningless and yet we have meaning. Universal Truth is often seemingly paradoxical, yet making perfect sense with those with ears to hear and eyes to see...

CHAPTER 5

Setting the Record Straight

~~~

Deeply humbled, grateful and awed.

This is my experience when I consider the great mysteries of Creation, spiritual initiation and the journey of evolution through time and space. How could I not be humbled in the face of such clear vision of my own insignificance, while feeling so loved and supported? How could I not be curious and grateful about the fact that I have a part to play in the great Universal dance?

Many people shy away from the experience of being humbled, often confusing it with that of being humiliated. I enjoy being reminded that I am but a small creature who lives as part of a larger Being, and that I am part of a complex, multi-dimensional, eternal, ordered Universe. It only makes my Soul adventure more exciting! While the ego always likes to be right, be in control and be the one to "know stuff", the humbled soul rejoices in the many things they have yet to learn, discover, explore and grow into. How boring to think that you are at the top of your game and have nothing more to learn? Where do you go from there? It's a dead end! And how arrogant to think of ourselves as the centre of Creation, the only intelligent life forms, or the apex of planetary evolution! The experience of a masterful Soul will always be that the more we learn and grow, the more we realise that we know nothing. I also hope that what we have explored so far has provided you with some insight into the amazing expansiveness of the Creation we are a part of, but also of the fullness of the journey of initiation.

There is an immense richness to this process called Life, which reaches through eternity and infinity. It is a huge journey indeed, one beyond the small human mind's ability to truly behold. The perfection, complexity and simplicity of the design of Creation are reflected in our bodies, our natural landscape and our eco-systems. We were spawned as part of this greater Divine Design, and we express as lower correspondences of the Whole: beautiful and miraculous in our own right, and yet so very small and insignificant within All That Is. This acknowledgement of our unique beauty and wonder, balanced with the knowing of our limited existence and individual insignificance in the grander scheme of things, is what can birth Humility. We exist by the good graces of the Soul Tree, and our choice to contribute evolutionary value. The world certainly does not owe us an existence. Life is a privilege.

Being Spiritual Does Not Make You Better Than Anyone Else: The Importance of Humility on the Spiritual Path

Many people confuse Humility with false modesty, thinking that to play small and play down one's abilities and qualities is humility. But Humility is not false modesty or putting one's self down. Humility is actually a state of holding a fine point of balance and proportion. It comes from truly acknowledging where one is at, no more, no less. It is accepting, but also allowing, ourselves to be exactly where we are at... with all the achievements behind us, and all the many things we do not yet know, and even the things we don't know that we don't know. We acknowledge our journey so far and its value, as well as how much more we have to go. We maintain an appropriate sense of perspective of our place within the greater scheme of things. Humility is, in some ways, the embodiment of one of those paradoxical spiritual truths whereby we celebrate how our existence and our journey matter, yet always remember how much we do not matter at the same time. To be truly humble is to be comfortable with our strengths and ability, yet also deeply aware of our shortcomings and ignorance. We do not take ourselves seriously because to do so would be egoic self-importance. In balance, to not take ourselves seriously does not mean that we treat ourselves as a joke; it simply means that we do not have an inflated ego, don't take everything personally, don't defend our bullshit when someone calls it out, or choose to feel insulted and outraged every time someone disagrees with our egoic reality. While we should not take ourselves seriously, the humbled initiate will certainly take their evolution and their service work seriously.

Humility is an important quality to nurture for ones on the path, because as the evolving disciple progresses on the spiritual path, it is a common trap to develop a sense of superiority and all knowing-ness. As I have shared, the masterful and humbled soul will experience the opposite: the more they learn, the more they realise what they did not know and so realise how little they know. Interestingly enough, as with most areas of expertise in life, it is often those who know the least who assume to know the most. This is called the Dunning-Kruger effect in psychology. It is a cognitive bias created by the fact that we do not know what we do not know, and so assume that our knowledge is all there is to know, while remaining blind to the scale of our ignorance. By learning a little bit of wisdom and having a few spiritual realisations, we may feel like they've discovered so much spiritual truth that it makes us instant experts in spiritual matters. Little do such people realise how small the volume of their spiritual exploration compared to the vastness of the Mind of God!

For those on the spiritual path, Humility is crucial. Spiritual pride and spiritual glamour are all too common among egos using spirituality to make themselves feel special or superior, because they see themselves as more evolved, or more spiritually gifted. There is only so far that we can go on the path of initiation by taking ourselves too seriously, or using spiritual work and spiritual energy to inflate our ego. This is a phenomenon called the spiritual ego: whereby one approaches the work of spiritual progression identified as a separate individual personality, rather than in service of the Soul. Instead of using their spiritual practices and experiences as tools to facilitate their surrendering to the control of the Soul and Oversoul, they try to direct and control their progression from egoic-self identification. They still experience some changes, yet mostly the ego learns by mimicking behaviour so that it can pretend to be spiritual, instead of allowing the Soul and Spirit to spiritualise it. Such disciples do not understand that the process of evolution is mostly one of undoing and unravelling everything which entombs the Divine spark within us. God is human minus ego. In order to realise God, we must learn to surrender and dissolve the egoic structure which keeps us separate from the unity with God, which is universally true.

We may progress and actualise up to a point on the path while carrying a lot of our egoic patterning. Yet unless we are thorough with clearing our psyche of fear and egoic-control, we can run into problems as the incoming spiritual energy clashes with the fear resonating within the lower bodies. Incoming spiritual energy floods our entire system and therefore illuminates and energises everything within us, including any remnants of fear and negative egoic programming. If we do not keep up with clearing out our negative ego patterning, we can develop various psychological, emotional and behavioural aberrations. We may begin to take ourselves too seriously, become filled with spiritual pride and spiritual glamour, become unstable, erratic or miserable. Spiritual pride is what happens when our spiritual achievements and experiences go to our head. We start to feel superior to those who are not on the spiritual path, looking down on them. This can lead to spiritual entitlement, feeling justified in self-righteously judging, expecting special treatment, taking advantage of other people, playing games of domination, or even putting down anyone who appears to be reaching near our level. This is what can cause spiritual abuse, whether sexual, psychological, emotional or financial. The corrupt initiate starts to think their shit does not stink, and act like the king of their little empire. This can cause great harm, especially when the corrupt initiate is in a position of power and influence. From that point, it is only a matter of time before that initiate falls off the initiation ladder, as the negative ego gains the upper hand and drives them back into spiritual unconsciousness. Remember, anyone call fall off the spiritual ladder - no matter how high they may have achieved- if they are not vigilant and holding themselves to high spiritual and ethical standards. There are no exceptions to the rule of maintaining spiritual standing: standards have to be upheld in all areas of mastery, or else we lose our standing as we spiral down with our unresolved fear.

The other common manifestation of a lack of humility for those on the path is spiritual glamour. While spiritual pride is a distortion of personal power on spiritual steroid, spiritual glamour is more a distortion of the emotional and feeling experience of one's spirituality. Both are interwoven, but have a different flavour. Glamour is a form of astral, or emotional, magic. It is the energy woven and generated by the ego when we are invested in a particular feeling that goes along with an imagined reality or narrative. It is a form of emotional intoxication as we get incensed by our own self-created bullshit, basically putting ourselves under an astral spell that makes us feel and appear a certain way. If we want other people to buy into our story and illusion, we can project and share our emotional illusion around so others come under our astral spell too. It is a form of emotional manipulation which can feel like a haze, or like an intoxication or a drug which energises your ego and may even feel good in the short term, but at a spiritual cost. Glamour is a form of lying, through emotional energy rather than words, in the same way that illusion is lying through mental beliefs and energy. Such weaving of energy is the basis for astral magic, which is the lowest form of magic and usually synonymous with the selfish magic which is dark magic. Someone full of spiritual glamour will also fancy themselves as something quite special, and feed on the adulation that others provide when they buy into the projected glamour. Such people tell themselves all sorts of stories about what makes them so special, thereby feeding their glamour-intoxication. They also become quite defensive to anyone daring to question their narratives or refusing to buy into their glamour. Questioning is perceived as a threat which could break the spell (including to themselves) because anyone who questions has not fallen under the spell. Anyone refusing to go along with their glamour will be rejected, belittled or demonised, and then stubbornly ignored.

A humbled initiate values and loves Truth. If we are wrong, we want to know. If we are deluded, we want our illusions shattered. Being disillusioned is a good thing, it means our illusions have been taken away! If we are in glamour, we want to come back to earth and get real. The trick is, it is hard to see our own bullshit. To help ourselves, we must notice the stark reflections of truth provided by the universe as she seeks to break through our illusions and glamours. These reflections will usually be the things in our lives which trigger us and cause us to want to defend and justify, while being emotionally charged. Everyone, to some degree, carries some egoic pride, glamour and illusion. The journey of enlightenment and growth into mastery involves many experiences of humiliation, disillusionment and sobering reality checks. If you truly want to achieve far in your spiritual evolution, you'd better buckle up and welcome these opportunities with open arms, for through such experience lies the door to more truth. If you hold on to the illusion of knowing everything and being right all the time, then you will not realise God. Accept that there is much you don't know yet and be open to changing your mind as you grow. Being proven wrong is part of the journey.

In the spirit of being a little less wrong, I would like to debunk certain illusions and distortions which I have commonly encountered among those on the spiritual path. Of course, anything I say could be wrong. All I can do is share honestly from my current level of knowing and understanding. It is up to your wise, open-minded discernment and deepest heart's knowing to decide if you, as a Soul, resonate with what I share and challenge here.

You Are Not The One Achieving Enlightenment, The Soul Is!

I know I have mentioned this before, but it bears repeating briefly. One useful remedy to the illness of spiritual ego is to remind one's self that it is not you, as a little personality or as a human creature, who is becoming a spiritual initiate or Master. Master souls are called Master Souls for a reason: It is the soul which achieves mastery, not the egoic separate self. The body-mind that you, as a soul, currently animate and inhabit, is but a vessel, and a point of focus into the physical plane. The human part of you will only ever be that: a human creature. The highest possible achievement that the human vehicle can reach is that of being a loving, wise, psychologically clear vessel who has surrendered him or herself to the control of Soul and Higher Self. Our lower bodies are part of the Earth and enable us to be here, incarnate within her and as a part of her and her evolution, as physical creatures. Our human vehicles also provide a channel through which the soul can undergo experience and evolution, and through which to contribute our soul wisdom to the collective learning of this humanity and the planet. For the most part, the job of the human personality in the spiritual process is to surrender, let go and get out of the way of the Soul. Once trained and mastered by the soul, the embodiment can give herself over to be guided, informed and a vessel for the Higher Self. No matter what level of initiation you may reach, it is hard to take your little self too seriously if you remember this simple fact.

The Tree decides when you become enlightened
Just as the human self is not the one becoming a Master Soul, it is also not up to the human self to decide when you undergo initiation or spiritual activation. All we can do, as human beings, is make ourselves ready by meeting the standards and benchmarks necessary for initiation and activation. We must make ourselves empty vessels. Empty of what? Empty of fear, empty of contraction and empty of egoic control. The emptied human vessel surrenders and waits to be filled by the presence and Knowing of the Soul Tree, all in Divine Timing. When and how this happens is above the paygrade of any human ego. Just like a job interview, all we can do is prepare ourselves and fit ourselves to the job role and what it requires. After that, it is up to the company doing the hiring, and the people interviewing

you, to decide if you are ready and a good fit. In the same way, each individual human embodiment, and each individual soul, can only make itself ready and fit for purpose, humbly and patiently being available in service of the Soul Tree. The Higher Self is the one that decides whether you actually meet the criteria and are ready for the next step in your evolution. We, as humans, can ask, pray and call to our Higher Self. But unless we make ourselves ready and fit for purpose, these calls cannot be properly answered because we have not made ourselves fit the Tree. It would be the height of arrogance and spiritual unconsciousness to demand that the Soul Tree shape itself to fit you! The leaf does not decide on behalf of the tree; it is the Tree who directs the overall growth pattern of the entire tree, as well as what happens with the leaves. Yet many spiritual seekers make this mistake and demand God meets them on their own terms, and in their own time. It does not work like that. If you want to enter the ranks of those who are awakened and working in spiritual service, then you must learn to take instruction from the Higher Self. You must become whoever and however the Soul Tree needs you to be, to be of use to the greater evolutionary purpose of both the Soul Tree and the planet.

Initiation and evolution are not usually a fast process. While the pace of our progression depends on how committed and willing to surrender we are, most Souls require hundreds, or even a thousand or more, incarnations in order to complete only one initiation. Given this fact, and the reality that our Higher selves are in charge of deciding when we are ready, it is obvious that no one else can simply make you go through major spiritual initiations at one of their weekend workshops. Nor can anyone else activate your higher light-bodies, or make you suddenly galactically activated, over a series six or even twelve workshops! Any spiritual teacher who makes such claim lacks humility and understanding of the depth and intricacy of the process of initiation. As you would have gathered by no, it takes long and hard work on one's self to attain such levels of activations.

A teacher can help you to prepare for initiation, share their wisdom and support you with their energy, and save you some time by offering guidance and protection. It is possible to partner and work with higher spiritual beings, advanced initiates or spiritual Masters in order to facilitate a certain degree of acceleration of this process. Under the committed long-term tutelage and energetic support of a Master, we can benefit from some degree of acceleration of the journey of spiritual initiation. Even for the outstanding soul retracing their steps from previous lives' achievements, it will take years of serious and consistent spiritual and psychological clearing work, and much testing, in order to progress through the elemental initiations. If the Soul is undergoing these initiations for the first time, it will take much longer. Even under the tutelage and support of a Master, a whole lifetime of committed spiritual and personal clearing work may barely be enough to go through one of the higher initiations. It is important to understand the difference between undergoing initiation for the first time in our Soul's journey versus retracing our steps in going over initiations achieved in previous lives. Initiations previously achieved by the Soul in other embodiments will be quicker to undergo as the disciple is basically repeating familiar territory and catching up to previously held levels of mastery and activation. When we are venturing into new evolutionary territory, however, the process of progression is much slower and arduous. If anyone promises to initiate you into some lofty spiritual status, or activate all these amazing higher bodies within a short amount of time, because you are coming to a workshop or retreat, run! They are false prophets. It is not up to us, let alone any other person, to decide when activation happens; it is up to the Soul

Tree. We all need teachers as no one can do it alone, but you still have to put in the hard yards every day in order to make yourself ready. The Soul Tree will guide you, if you will but be receptive. You must shape yourself to become a suitable vessel for the energy of the Soul Tree to focus on you, and through you, and inform your existence. As a person, you must give yourself over to be the Servant of the Higher Self, in, of and for Love, in service to All That Is. This is the order of Creation, and no catchy marketing or glamourous spiritual claims can change this.

Spiritual Masters are not perfect
No one is perfect.

Yet, the more spiritually evolved and enlightened we are, the less character weaknesses we have and sign of poor character eventually disappear from the expression of the Spiritual Master. One cannot achieve spiritual Mastery or high advancement in the initiation process while still being prone to things like selfishness, jealousy, envy, terror, vengefulness, cowardice, being mean-spirited or cruel. Anyone who is still a slave to their physical urges, fears and carnal hedonistic needs has not even fully met the criteria for the first initiation. Anyone who is a slave to the vagaries of their emotions or held hostage to the demands of their emotional needs has not achieved full mastery of the second initiation yet. A beginner, kindergarten level Spiritual Master within a planetary context is one who has entered well into the fifth initiation. You may revisit our chapter on the process of initiation if you wish to remind yourself of the criteria to achieve this level of spiritual initiation. At this stage, a certain amount of physical, emotional and mental control and discipline have been achieved by the Soul, within an orientation of love towards humanity and the planet, and in selfless service to the process of evolution. As such, many nasty traits and human weaknesses seen in the common man will not be so readily witnessed in the spiritual master. Yet, the Master is still a work in progress, still continuing to clear their karmic load, still having to face their self-imposed limitations and ignorance, and still improving themselves. No one knows everything, and no one is perfect; yet some are more refined, loving, enlightened, masterful and wise than other. Those who have attained to higher levels of expansion will hold a different reality to those who have not, as their consciousness includes several planes and dimensions and access to greater Knowing. As such, more advanced Souls have more refined character, more spiritual control of all aspects of themselves and a more expansive and connected perspective. Yet, they are not perfect. This is important for spiritual students to remember, as many often approach a Master Teacher with these unrealistic expectation of absolute abiding perfection in every tiny way.

What one needs from a Spiritual Teacher is a demonstration that they are a few steps ahead of you in what you are seeking to learn, are the real deal (rather than a false prophet blowing their own trumpet). They must be ethical and seek to empower not themselves but you. They must also seek to empower you as the Soul, rather than your ego. This can be challenging for junior students who struggle with having enough confront to face the uncomfortable reflections aimed at dissolving the control of the negative ego.

Anyone can't be your Spiritual Teacher

In a philosophical sense, everyone and every experience in your life can be your spiritual teacher, because every encounter and experience is an opportunity to learn something, practice your mastery and your capacity to be wise, loving, courageous and spiritually intelligent.

In more literal terms, while you are free to choose anyone you wish to become your spiritual teacher, there are a few things to take into consideration if you want the partnership to be useful and successful.

Firstly, the teacher or Master must also accept you. Regardless of how much you want to study with a particular Master or teacher, if they feel you are not ready or not well-suited to their approach, they absolutely have right of refusal. It is only an entitled ego who would demand acceptance for spiritual teaching by a Master regardless of what the Master feels about the applicant's readiness. If you are not accepted but wish to be, then all you can do is to humbly and seriously work on yourself in order to become ready.

Secondly, there is no point in learning from someone who is not ahead of you in the process of God realisation, and whose vibration is not more refined than yours. Would you seek piano lessons from someone who plays less well than you do? Would you ask for relationship advice from someone who has no track record of successful relationships? Only a fool would do so! If you wish to progress on the path, you must be supported and guided by ones who have already achieved what you seek to achieve, and whose energy will uplift you, not drag you down vibrationally. Such teachers can, from their own lived experience and actualised knowing, support you to follow in their footsteps. Anyone who teaches what they, themselves, have not integrated and actualised can only offer you theoretical understanding. Such teachings can be interesting and entertaining to the mind, but carry no real spiritual substance or transformational potential. You must, at any given stage of your spiritual evolution, seek guidance and support only from those who demonstrate that they are indeed ahead of you in the process you seek to master.

Even by following this precept, it may mean that you end up working with more than one teacher over your lifetime, especially if you grow fast or are recapitulating the attainment from other soul-leaves incarnations, which is a faster process. Sometimes, we are drawn into particular relationships for a time in our lives. We may get much out of these relationships, but eventually we feel like we are done with what these relationships contributed to our journey, or we outgrow the people we were with. It is the same for a relationship with spiritual teachers. Sometimes, especially in the earlier stages of the journey of reawakening in our life, we travel alongside a particular teacher, or follow a set of teachings, for a time. This helps us at that stage of our growth, but eventually we become ready to move on to the next evolutionary stage of our journey. In the same way, we may feel drawn to work with people, whether spiritual or not, who have expertise in a particular area. Our association with them is more narrowly focused on learning from them in their area of expertise, but not necessarily in any other way. A good example of this would be to hire the services of a qualified and successful health coach in order to help you master your physical habits and foster physical health and well-being. While you can learn much about physical self-care and discipline from such a person, this does not mean that they qualify to teach you in areas other than their area of expertise. Reversely, a Spiritual Master is a master of the craft of spiritual evolution, timeless wisdom and spiritual service. But this does not make them experts at everything either. Ask a Spiritual Master a few questions about woodwork, or playing the piano, and you may find that some have answers for you and some don't. A spiritual Master worth their salt will try to learn a bit about most things, as this is part of being well-rounded and integrated in one's mastery. A Master can also access a certain amount of Knowing through channelling from the collective experience and wisdom of all the various leaves of the Soul Tree. They can only do this to the degree of their achievement of oneness identification with a good portion of their Soul Tree. No one in incarnate form can know or do everything, however, and no one is infallible.

While our life and spiritual journey may meander to associate with a number of people, groups and teachers, you must be mindful to not fall into the trap of being the fickle little spiritual bee that flits from flower to flower. Such hopping about from one teacher or tradition to another, without ever staying the course, is more about a fear of commitment, fear of hard-work, and the hedonistic chasing of the honey-moon phase excitement we feel when we discover something new. Everyone spends a certain amount of time searching for their path; this is both normal and healthy. Yet, any Soul truly committed to moving forward with their evolution and initiation journey will eventually be guided to the "right" teacher, and must then commit in the long term in order to get results. Fleeting from spiritual flower to spiritual flower may be fun and free, and appropriate for the spiritual beginner or aspirant. But please open your hearts and minds to be guided to and recognise when you have finally found the path and teacher your Soul Tree was looking for. This is what happened to me. I spend years in my late teens and early adulthood searching for a path, through the reading of books, my time spent at the British Museum, attending spiritual workshops, mediumship courses, new age fairs and conferences. I visited crop circles with like-minded strangers and took part in shamanic retreats, healing courses and meditation groups. I learnt and gained something from all of it, yet I also knew that they were not quite "it", not quite what I felt called to. When I finally discovered my tribe and the right path, I just knew I had finally found what I was looking for. I committed right then and there, and never looked back.

You Can't Do It All Yourself and Find Your Own Way to Ascend.

No one can do it all by themselves. While we may explore, experiment with different teachings, read many books and create our own version of a spiritual path for a time, there is only so far we can go without committing to one path, and finding a teacher and group of other disciples and initiates.

There have been specific ways and paths to Ascension which were designed based on spiritual truth, and have become long-established based on their proven success, over many thousands of years. Paths towards Ascension are like finely tuned recipes, where the ingredients are the panoply of tools, practices, disciplines, attitudes and alignments of that particular path or tradition. At some point, the flitting and experimentation must stop, and the seeker must commit to a given recipe. Mixing up bits and pieces of different traditions can only take you so far. The recipe for a delicious chocolate cake does not work so well if you start adding beef and broccoli to it. There is nothing wrong with beef and broccoli, but they don't work in a chocolate cake. It is the same for spiritual practice; the mix of ingredients have to be just right to work together. The paradigm, tools and techniques of different spiritual paths don't necessarily work together.

Doing it all alone is not an option either. Initiation is, ultimately, a group process. The more one advances through the stages of initiation, the more the work becomes about unity, group consciousness and functioning as part of a greater whole. This is not true only in spiritual terms, but also in a grounded manner in our day-to-day lives. The embodied Soul retracing its steps and recapitulating previous spiritual attainment may, up to a point, do so with only the assistance of the invisible, inner-plane spirit mentors which support all disciples and initiates on the path. Our invisible support team will be able to help us undergo the familiar learning and testing associated with initiations undergone many times in previous incarnations. As soon as we get into less practiced territory, or into brand new territory, we need to call to and seek our teacher in the flesh. As the ancient, well-known adage goes: when the student is ready, the teacher will appear. It is then up to the student to pass the test of recognition (Do you recognise your true teacher when you meet him or her?), the test of discernment (Is this presenting teacher the real deal or a false prophet? Is this teacher the one that's right for me?), and the test of boundaries (Am I going to let my ego or the egos of others get in the way of my committing to my path and teacher?).

But hear me out: no one can do it alone, no one ever has. It is the ancient way.

The Question of Sex

Sex is a wonderful aspect of human experience. It is not only a means of biological reproduction for Earth creatures, but also a means of communicating love and affection with another person. Sex is also a much, much lower correspondence expression of the act of Primordial Creation between the Masculine-Transmitting and Feminine-Receptive aspects of Unified Source, from which all Creation came into being. The human act of sexual union can create new human life. The Primordial act of Creation between God and Goddess was a creation of great Cosmic love and light. In order for our sexual expression to be in harmony with our Divine Nature and the spiritual essence of the larger Being we are a part of, our sexuality must also be an expression of great love and light, within self and with the other person.

Sadly, the way our world approaches sex can be more about carnal appetites and selfish pleasure than genuine, mutual love, respect and joy. Looking back over humanity's history until now, sex has been a minefield of primal animalistic urges, power games, shame, abuse, enslavement, manipulation, neediness and desperation. The evil business of human trafficking for sex is worth many millions of dollars in profit each year, and drunken casual sex with strangers on weekends is way too common an occurrence in the West. Sex performed in anything less that mutual love, care, joy and respect is destructive to the spiritual progress of the Soul. I am not saying two people wishing to have sex with each other must be absolutely in love for the encounter to be spiritually healthy. Two friends can have spiritually healthy sex, as long as there is mutual care, respect and joy between them, and as long as both participants approach the act with love. A healthy friendship or professional relationship can easily be complicated and even destroyed by introducing sex into the equation, however. The decision of having sex with someone should never be a decision made lightly for the spiritual disciple.

Sex has permanent energetic repercussions beyond that of affecting our vibration. The act of sex establishes permanent energetic cords between the sacral chakra of the two people involved. Cords are the energetic connections between us and other people we have relationships with. Most cords can be severed and dissolved at will, if we choose to disconnect from the other person. Some cords, however, cannot be dissolved. This includes genetic cords which connect you directly with your parents, and in a more indirect way to your siblings. Genetic cords connect into every one of our chakras, are established from birth and cannot be severed. Sexual cords connect into the sacral chakra around the reproductive area in the lower abdomen, and cannot be severed either. This means that anyone you have sex with, regardless of the circumstance, is someone you will have a permanent energetic connection with for the rest of your life. Permanent cord connections can be cleansed, and boundaries can be held within them, but they only dissolve when one of the people corded dies.

Casual loveless sex is basically people using each other like pieces of meat that they hump, to scratch an animalistic itch. Such a carnal act, giving in to our lower nature, will bring our vibration down in dramatic ways, and connect us for life to complete strangers. Hate sex, sex which is used to dominate another, or sex which is about seeking relief from one's pain, loneliness or emptiness will also erode our vibration and energetic purity. Any sexual practice which is about pain, fear-based need, power over, carnality or selfish hedonism is the expression of internal malaise, not that of a radiant Soul.

I am sure you can all feel the difference between sexual energy which is creepy, or about using you, and sexual energy from a person who truly loves and respects you. Sex is ultimately just a tool, a vehicle to express love towards each other, to please and uplift each other. If the energies shared and expressed through the sex act are impure, selfish, angry, self-pitying, fearful, insecure, or rattled with pain, then you are basically inviting all these lower vibrational energies right into your system. This can cause great havoc to the refined vibration of a spiritual initiate. Too much of this for too long and you can do yourself actual damage up even to soul level. In the same way, having sex with people whose energy vibrates at a much lower level than yours will also fill you up with lower vibrational energy, draining your vibration throughout your four-body system. Bluntly put: a refined, evolved soul should not have sex with rough, unevolved humans.

I will add a comment here for those you may have been sexually assaulted or abused in the past. Anyone who was forced against their will into a sexual act without mutual love will need to undergo a thorough process of recovery, healing and clearing; but this is not the same as you willingly inviting and engaging with loveless sex. Our degree of openness to the other person during the act makes a difference too. One may have lovely sex and yet remain relatively closed to their partner's energy, while others may be willing to be energetically open to anyone they have sex with. Boundaries and levels of openness during sex does mitigate the effects of the encounter to a point. While loveless sex will not be good for you spiritually, it will not cause the same amount of damage as it would in someone happily abandoning themselves to the experience. To be honest, if you were abused or assaulted, other factors will have as much of an effect on your energy and vibration as that of the assault itself. Your attitude post-assault is key. Many things will need to be felt, moved through and released but I suggest you don't let the bastards get you down! Feel and clear out the pain and trauma, but don't wallow in shame or self-pity, don't become bitter, don't let fear win. This is something that happened to you, but it does not define you. It was an event, nothing more, and it is now in the past. You survived, you are here, and you can heal and recover and live to fight another day. The best is yet to come. Process all the feelings that come from the experience, but give yourself permission to move on. Don't let it cost you more than it needs to. While the act of sex itself has consequences in how it affects us, our own attitude and judgment towards it can also do damage. Learn from the past, but do not hold yourself prisoner to it.

The act of sex between two people of a roughly similar bandwidth of vibration, and who love, enjoy, care for and respect each other, can be a great way to fill each other with love and joy, and to express affection for each other. Remember that sexual energy is, ultimately, just creative energy. The same rush you may feel after orgasmic sex is the same type of rush an artist may feel when suddenly inspired and filled with new creative ideas. It is simply a different level of expression of the same energy: One is physical, the other more mental and emotional. Any willingly embraced sexual act can give you that rush of creative energy as it flows through your body, a sort of buzz if you will. It's just nature responding. Experiencing this rush does not mean it was necessarily good sex, that you are in love. Some people seek sexual connections as a means to fill an emotional void or a lack of self-esteem. Sex is like a drug for them, momentarily making them feel wanted, connected and worthy. I have seen people like this feel a sort of high after having sex with others who did not love them, and confusing the basic sexual orgasmic rush with love. This is generally more common in women, for whom orgasm is deeply linked with the emotional bonding response due our ability to become pregnant. The rush of physical magnetic attraction and desire, and the explosion of physical creative orgasmic energy, provides momentary relief and high. Eventually, as the rush passes, the person comes back down to Earth and feels they need more. This is, of course, the dynamic behind sex addiction.

Ultimately, anyone truly committed to the spiritual path must transcend both extremes of their relationship with sex: their hang-ups and their obsession. Most average people think about sex a lot: how to have it, how not to have it, wanting it, not wanting it, loving it, hating it, seeking it, pushing it away, weighing the sexual attractiveness of everyone they meet, scanning for potential sexual partners everywhere they go, and wanting to appear sexually attractive to everyone else. It is one of the major preoccupations of the average person. And yet, it is such a small part of the entire human and spiritual experience available to us! The high level spiritual initiate and the Spiritual Masters do not place such important on sex, because their inner life and their world is so much bigger than that. If they are in a mutually loving relationship, then they enjoy sex with their partner when they have it, and don't obsess about it when they don't. If they don't have a partner, it's not a big deal because they do not define themselves by basic traits like their sexuality. If they pleasure themselves, it is from a place of self-love, self-respect and circulating the healing creative energy released by orgasm around their body and up to their hearts. They don't need sex, but they don't have hang-ups about it either. Sex becomes a complete non-issue. Obviously, self-respecting Masters and initiates do not normally engage in casual sex, because it is extremely rare to have a truly intimate, mutually loving, caring, respectful and joyful encounter with a complete stranger. The risk of lower energies being introduced into their field is too high. A Master avoids the touch of a hand that does not love them.

As far as the relationship between spiritual teachers and their students go, some teachers seem to think that having sex with their students is a perfectly good way to share the spiritual energy, transcendent love and Knowing they wish to impart to their charges. I strongly disagree with such practices in spiritual groups.

First, such acts are too often a poor excuse for the unintegrated teacher to take advantage of the adulation of his followers for his own selfish sexual gratification. To me, this is the equivalent of spiritual incest, and is absolutely reproachable. Second, sex is a minefield of shame, trauma, pain, hang ups and neediness driven by low self-esteem. While I will admit that yes, it is not completely beyond the infinite realm of possibilities that a truly masterful, clear, absolutely selfless and disinterested spiritual teacher *could* theoretically share with a student of his energy, love and reality through the communion of the sexual act, the chances of confusion and harm being caused in the process would way outweigh any potential benefit. There are obviously a plethora of other ways to impart Knowing, love and enlightenment which are more natural, straightforward and empowering to the students. Why resort to sex when it often causes more harm, confusion and personal entanglement than it's worth? Contrary to many other spiritual groups, I and my colleagues at the Cosmosis® Mentoring Centre have a clear policy of no sex or romantic relationships between teachers and students. To do so constitutes a severe breach of our Code of Ethics and Professional Conduct. Sexual entanglements between teachers and students are not based on equality, and they confuse the boundaries between the personal and the professional. Ultimately, all this gets in the way of the spiritual work of the teaching. It is, as far as we are concerned, a no-no and a form of spiritual abuse.

Raising your Kundalini or Spinning the Merkaba is Not Enough

The Merkaba (sometimes spelt Merkabah) is a geometric energetic structure which is part of our light-body structure and houses the light of the Soul. It is shaped like two opposite three-sided pyramids – one facing up and one facing down - which interlock to form a three-dimensional six-pointed start. The kundalini is an energy which rises from the base of the spine in response to spiritual activation. Some spiritual and yogic practices and techniques aim to force the raising of the kundalini's energy up the spine to activate the various chakras along our central energy column. There are also some practices designed to "spin" the Merkaba's tetrahedrons in order to draw energy from both Earth and Heaven to balance masculine and feminine energies within us, and accelerate our spiritual activation. I do not recommend such practices because, like any other shortcut options on the spiritual path, it is trying to force and trick a process which should be allowed to occur in its natural manner and timing. When an evolving soul undergoes the spiritual work of psychological clearing, energy purification, behavioural and character refinement, self-mastery, and surrendering to the control and guidance of their Higher Self, their energy system will gradually and naturally change, activate and adapt. As the disciple undergoes the realigning and transformation of the initiation process, the kundalini and many other energetic activations will unfolds all of their own accords. When these processes unfold naturally and in divine timing, as the evolving soul does the required work to earn their way up the evolutionary ladder, the energetic activation are safe, happening as they are meant to be by Nature's design. The psychological clearing is a huge part of what prepares an initiate to undergo these energetic activations naturally and safely. Using trick practices or substances to try to force, shortcut or highjack energetic activation without doing the proper work of psychological clearing, spiritual control and purification of character can be dangerous for body and mind. Beyond the risk to one's health and psychological balance, it is also literally a form of cheating the system and there is no honour in that. Everything that goes around, comes around.

A Master may use certain techniques to move energy around their four-body system, to vivify and balance certain energy points and allow energetic flow. This is simply part of energetic self-care. It is not the same as the uninitiated trying to force their way into activation they have not earned fairly. As for every choice, there are consequences. I have heard of initiates causing great damage to themselves mentally or physically, by using such tricks without doing the proper purification work. The best approach is always to do the work of clearing and self-mastery, and allow activation to happen naturally as we make ourselves ready.

The Question of Drugs and Alcohol

The use of substances to achieve an altered state allowing us to reach into the "other world" is ancient and rooted in the shamanic practices of earlier civilisations. It remains a popular approach to transcendent experiences among the seekers of the new age movement, but I do not recommend the use of drugs for anyone serious about the achievement of spiritual mastery. Like sex, this can be a tricky topic, as it usually triggers people's attachment to the easy ways to get off and shortcut our way into spiritual experiences. I understand the effect that certain drugs have on the human mind and energy system, and how they can momentarily alter our perceptions, open our minds and awaken our senses. This may allow us to tap into the otherworldly and the self-transcendent for a short series of moments, as these substances alter the chemical balance in our bodies. Changes in our body's chemistry affect our brain and our glands, which are linked to the chakra system. Chakras are how the Soul interfaces with the lower bodies. Substances like drugs and alcohol affect the relationship between soul and body, and momentarily remove certain boundaries within our minds. I have seen some people have their worldviews expanded through the use of natural plant psychedelics in particular. These experiences led them to consider existence and reality beyond the confines of the five physical senses. Yet, I have also seen people become damaged by drugs, and ruin their chances at any serious spiritual attainment in this life; in some cases they ruined their chances at success at all. Ancient traditional shamanic practices rely not only on the ingestion of hallucinogenic plants, but also psychological and spiritual purification and preparation before the experience. This type of conscious approach, integrated into actual spiritual work, tends to facilitate a more meaningful experience of self meeting self, or of communion with the otherworldly. Even then, most people access only a conscious experience of the astral plane, which is hardly pure or elevated. In all cases, the transcendent experience is short-lived, leaving only (if we're lucky) the memories of what we perceived, and perhaps a changed belief structure. No lasting fundamental enlightenment or mastery ensues from the use of drugs. For the average drug consumer, the taking of substances is approached hedonistically, as a way to "get out of it". Only destructiveness can come out of this.

Regular use of such drugs over time will cause damage and leave a murky etheric residue in one's field. You must understand that the taking of hallucinogenic drugs temporarily removes the usual boundaries and structures present in our mind and psyche. This allows perception through the higher senses of realities beyond the third dimension. At the end of the drug high, the boundaries and structures of the mind must fall back into place, but they do not always fall back in the same way that it was before. This may cause loss or muddling of memory and create mental fragmentation. In more fragile psyches, psychedelic experiences can leave them mentally, and sometimes emotionally scattered. It's as if things were not put back in the right order. I have known people who, through too much regular use of drugs like ecstasy, acid and cocaine, ended up damaged, splintered in their minds, and their nervous system twitchy and restless. It is undeniable that these substances can overload the unprepared nervous system and mind, and have a damaging effect on the physical body and the other lower bodies. Some people are more robust than others in handling the short-terms effects, and some individuals should simply never do drugs at all or risk immediate damage. In any case, I don't think anyone can claim that ingesting chemicals on a regular basis is a good idea for anyone, and certainly not for those committed to personal and spiritual purification. I find it funny to see people who eat clean, vegan, avoid chemicals in their homes or toiletries but happily ingest chemical poison twice a month at parties… there is a sort of dissonance and hypocrisy in this. In addition, chemically produced drugs always carry the risk of being cut with dangerous substances, without anyone knowing it. All of these risks and potential harm is not worth it if we seek proper enlightenment. Spiritual initiates do not consciously choose to cause harm to themselves just to get off or escape their lives. They work hard to make their body a clear temple for Spirit. The use of recreational drugs just does not support this.

From a more spiritual perspective, the use of drugs like psychedelics and ecstasy can also actually affect the natural receptors in the brain which are activated with peak spiritual experiences. These receptors are, by natural design, meant for the release of neurochemicals when the embodied Soul is having a true spiritual transcendent experience. Any initiate progressing on the path will, at some point in their journey, have profound experiences of glimpsing and entering into perception of the otherworldly and the higher planes. These peak experiences are meant to happen naturally as the initiate enters into higher dimensional states, as a result of their spiritual practices, purifying their psyche, aligning themselves to their Soul Tree, expanding their consciousness and being receptive. Deep meditation or participation in spiritual processes can sometimes bring encounters with other dimensional beings of light, meaningful visions, deep feelings of love and all sorts of transcendent experiences. As spiritual epiphanies occur, neuro-chemicals are released, which are a natural human version of the fake chemicals contained in some drugs. These epiphanies are the real deal though, not a cheat induced momentarily through the manipulation of our body chemistry. The genuine spiritual epiphany causes the neurotransmitter reaction, whereas drugs fabricate an artificial neurotransmitter reaction to try to reproduce or force a spiritual epiphany. It's upside down. The drug experience will induce the phenomena, but not the essence of the spiritual epiphany experience. The initiate earns their multi-dimensional experiences through spiritual practice and working on themselves. As a result, the initiate is fundamentally changed as a result. The trippy quality of the initiate's experience is simply the by-product of their transformation, not the cause. Not so for the drug user, who is like a spectator: they may have learnt something, they may remember it, but it does not transform them on a deep and real level like it does for the spiritual initiate.

Another major problem is that the drugs affect, reshape and often damage the synaptic receptors meant for the natural neurotransmitters of enlightenment and spiritual activation. This means that someone who overused drugs will have changed their brain to adapt to the fake chemical version of these molecules, to the point of no longer being receptive to the natural neurotransmitters of genuine spiritual peak experiences. This is a major cost to the spiritual initiate. This and the fact that shortcuts are just cheating, never leading to long-term success, is why I do not recommend the use of drugs as a way to tap into higher dimensions. No real enlightenment can be reached and held from the use of substances. If it was that easy, any idiot could become an enlightened Master! Only consistent spiritual practice and purification on every level of the self will lead you to genuine enlightenment and mastery. Stop trying to cheat the system!

As for alcohol, its deleterious effects on physical and mental health, as well as on social relationships, are now well documented. Drinking alcohol is a long-established part of our culture, but this does not mean it's good for us. No one who is well-informed these days can argue that alcohol is harmless. Drinking something which is basically a mild poison is not self-loving or wise. Not only do a number of our brain cells die every time we consume alcohol, but alcohol also prevents soul control of the lower bodies. This is why drunk people can so often behave in animalistic ways: all their lower urges and desires -be them sexual arousal, tribal euphoria or violence- take the upper hand as the soul cannot maintain control of a drunk body. The drunk body-mind wakes up the next day, either not remembering what they did the night before–which should be a serious red flag!–or feeling terrible both physically and mentally because of alcohol's poisonous effects. Alcohol numbs our senses, damages our brain, overloads our liver, and disconnects us from Soul, none of which is a spiritual Master would choose!

Alcohol is a poison, which is why it affects our bodies as it does, and too much of it can lead to alcohol poisoning. Alcohol is also a preservative. If you want to preserve fruit or other biological substances, one way to do so is to keep them in alcohol. Anyone seeking to progress as efficiently as possible on the spiritual path will need to change and adapt constantly, on every level of their being. The consumption of alcohol will create resistance to change in the body, preventing physical adaptation to higher vibrations of spiritualising energy and the transformation that comes with spiritual activation.

In the end, if you require substances that alter the chemistry in your bodies in order to feel good, be happy or have expansive experiences, then you are not in mastery of yourself. These are all crutches and cheats, all of which come with a cost to physical, mental and spiritual health in the long term. If you are truly serious about spiritual initiation and achievement of self-mastery in this lifetime, you will give up (or avoid) the use of drugs and alcohol. This is the only way towards true, long-lasting and integrated spiritual mastery.

You Have Free Will But You Can't Do Whatever You Want

Beings who do not have free will, like Angelics and Elohim, have their choices and behaviours guided solely by their prime Divine directive and function. They cannot deviate from their original purpose and function within our evolutionary Universe. Everything that they are, be and do is a direct expression of the purpose and function they were created to fulfil.

A being who has free will is, at its most basic, a being who has the capacity to choose between following the highest call of their Divine purpose, or choose something else entirely. If they do not choose to follow the call of higher love, then they can basically choose any other choice lesser than that. Ultimately, translated into simpler terms, free will is the ability to make choices which are not the highest choice available. In even simpler terms, free will is therefore the ability to make stupid choices.

We can make stupid choices, and it is our God-given right! The whole point is, of course, for Source to explore realms of possible choices and experiences, and to learn from it all, through us. I am sure we've all had experiences of going out into the world, to have a go at something we knew little about. We faced certain situations, we had to make choices, and we learnt through trial and error. Even though we initially had no idea what we were doing, the very act of making even stupid choices and figuring out what works and what doesn't is what ultimately makes us competent. As above, so below. Our experience is in the image of Source. Just like we grow through trial and error, so does the Source of All Life. Other life streams, who do not have free will, have a different job to do: they keep the wheels of Creation turning and the functions of the Divine Engine working, while us creatures are given the freedom to experiment with how to drive it. But even free will has its limits...

The unconscious, separate ego perceives itself as the centre of its little world, like a small child would. Ego does not realise that our very existence is granted to us by our Source, and that our free will has conditions placed on it by a Being beyond our capacity to truly comprehend. Free will was not given to creatures so they could go around destroying other parts of Creation. Everything exists because of an intention of Unified Source to express and explore itself across many planes and dimensions of existence. We only exist to contribute to this grand Cosmic project of Source-Self-exploration and evolution. Like everything else in existence, our free will has a function and is expected to work within the scope of the greater purpose of Creation. There would be no point in giving creatures free will unless it was meant to function as part of the greater plan. A little bit of risk exploring the unknown, and even a bit of chaos, does not scare Source as long as it is interesting in evolutionary terms. Yet, when unruly leaves abuse their free will to make choices which prove destructive to the plan, free will quickly finds its boundary.

As I have said before, Source is a patient parent, but not infinitely so. Regardless of what free-will creatures choose, the ultimate purpose and destination of this great Creational experiment was already decided, long before either you or I were even a twinkle in God's eyes. Whether we like it or not, we are part of a Creation that is evolving and seeks to realise it greatest potential of being and expression. We exist inside this larger purpose, and our free will is completely and absolutely conditioned by these parameters. Regardless of how we choose to use our free will, it will always feed into this pre-existing grand design of evolution. Regardless of what we choose from the vast array of potential choices available to us, the ultimate destination of our journey remains the same: evolution and return to Source. No matter what we do, the Universe will always feed our choices back to us in a form designed to steer us towards the ultimate evolutionary goal and destination for this Creation. We don't have a choice about the destination, we only have a choice about how we get there, and to some degree how long we take to get there. But, whichever long or short path we choose, our journey must bring value to Divine exploration and learning. This is why we exist; this is why our free will exists. If, over long periods of time, we use our free will in ways which do not contribute value to the ultimate Plan and Purpose, we become redundant. If, over time, we use our free in ways detrimental to Plan and Purpose, then we become a problem. There are consequences to both. Everything we are, and everything available for us to choose from, exists only by the grace of God. Our Soul Trees are the doormen of the Plan, managing us, their soul extensions, in order to keep their own evolutionary contribution on track within our greater Universe. It can take some time and many stupid free-will choices to be deemed a problem serious enough to be dealt with by higher levels of the Tree or Forest, but push your luck for too long and your abuse of the privilege of free will quickly backfire.

Free will is not a right, it is a privilege. The evolved Soul understands that choice is a powerful thing, and that every choice has consequences. The fact that every choice we make will, in due time, bear consequences is part of how the Universe tries to steer us towards making better choices. Do you have the free will to make any available choice you fancy? Yes, you do. But there will be consequences. If your choices bring value to the Plan and Purpose of your Soul Tree, and of Source, then you will receive graceful consequences. If your choices don't play nice with the previously agreed evolutionary goals and purpose for this planet and Creation, you won't like the consequences you get. The question you need to ask yourself is: How am I using my free will? To partner with Source? or to misbehave to please myself? When faced with a choice you know is not the highest choice available to you, ask yourself: Do I want to make this choice enough that I am willing to suffer for it? To cause harm by it? To be a destructive influence within Creation because of it? Think before you choose, because you must be willing and ready to take the consequences. Caring about the consequences of our choices and the desire to avoid causing harm is a hallmark of the evolved Soul. The desire to avoid causing harm can't become a paralysing fear, however (stopping you from making any choice in case it is harmful), but considering and foreseeing the likely consequences of our actions is an important aspect of Mastery.

Regardless of the choices we make, we will all end up evolving, and we will all end up at the same destination at the end of this Divine adventure. Our free will does not extend to choosing our ultimate eternal purpose; we only have free will about which path we choose to get there. This is the boundary to our free will. This does not mean we have to make perfect choices all the time. There is no such thing as perfection; there is only the willingness to do our best and make progress, overall. We all make mistakes, and that's part of learning and contributing to the evolution of All Life. All we can do is give it our best shot, make the wisest choices we can, and learn from the consequences.

Time Is Not An Illusion

It's not, but I understand what people mean by this. It is a distortion, and an oversimplification, of the understanding of multidimensionality.

If we look at it a certain way, we could say everything is an illusion. We are all just thought forms in the Mind of God, so perhaps we are all just divine imaginings. That may be true from a certain perspective, and yet we exist. We are having real experiences, which have real consequences in a Creation which also exists. Whatever the ultimate nature of that existence, we do exist. The materiality of third-dimensional experience is only one limited dimension of experience among many. Some people translate that to mean that it is an illusion, because it is a limited perspective of reality. This is incorrect. Perceiving only a small part of reality does not make that small part an illusion. If you look at one wall of a room, you are not seeing the other walls, but that does not make the wall you are looking at an illusion. The wall is real. The conclusions and meaning you may be drawing from seeing only one wall, however, may lead you to conceive of an illusory reality. If you perceive only a small chunk of reality, but assume you are seeing all of reality, and draw your life conclusions from this, then you are living in illusion. This is the subtlety and nuance of it.

Time as we experience it in the third-dimension is also real, although different to the experience of time on other dimensions. The linear passage of time is made possible by our energy being fixed in matter, and our experience being facilitated through the five physical senses. On higher planes and dimensions of consciousness, time is experienced as a flow, as a unity, as an is-ness, and beyond as dimensional experience becomes timeless.

Our experience of the flow of time results from the movement of consciousness through space. Take a moment to think about it: what gives us a sense of time passing? What is a day, as a unit of time? You can count one day in terms of minutes or hours, but these are arbitrary measures human minds created to divide and count the passage of time. In real-world terms, we know one day because of the movement of the sun through our sky and our transit through the darkness of night. Our experience of the passage of time is generated by the movement of our planet upon its axis, creating the cycles of day and night. Our experience of a year is created by the rotation of our planet around the sun. In the old days, before clocks, watches or calendars, humans marked the passage of the hours by the movement of the sun, and the passage of the month by the cycle of moon. The passage of the year was marked both by the rising point of the sun and by the change of the seasons. The passage of larger segments of time was gauged by the movements of the stars in our sky. Movement and change create our sense of time. This in itself carries a profound truth about Life itself: it is all about movement and change, or in other words, evolution. Change is the only certainty in life.

As humans learnt to create systems to count and quantify what they were observing, they noticed patterns. They used this knowledge to create calendars and clock-like ways of measuring portions of a day. But these quantifications are not factually real. No one can see an hour, or a minute and they don't exist in nature. They are concepts. You may say: "But what about the ticks of our clocks?" But the clock is a human-made construct, not a natural reality. Even our clocks mark the passage of time because of its movement in space: the clock's arms moving around its face, the movements of the gears within its mechanism, or a repetitive impulse into a piece of quartz. Even the instruments which count our time do so by tracking a cyclic, ever-changing yet repetitive movement and change.

So how can our personal experience of time be so subjective? The passage of one hour can seem like an eternity if we are bored or stuck in unpleasantness; yet happy times seem to pass in the blink of an eye! Doesn't that show us that time is an illusion? Not really. It shows us that the orientation of our own consciousness affects our experience of time, but this does not negate the existence of linear time passing. Regardless of our personal experience, there is a design construct which enables time to express as linear as it moves through the third-dimensional plane of existence. Our perception varies based on our state of being because our experience of linear time is a function of the flow of consciousness through space. Our consciousness and that of our Soul Tree flows through us as we exist and move in space. This gives us our experience of linear time speeding or slowing. We are therefore back to the notion of time being created by change and movement (of consciousness) through space. When our consciousness expands to exist on higher planes of experience, our subjective experience of time also changes because our consciousness changes. Yet, every plane we live within still have their own rules and design independently of us.

Life is Not a Fairy-Tale

Earth life is a school meant to facilitate evolution. To embrace both the agony and the ecstasy of living is a central part of achieving enlightenment and god realisation here. A heart that loves deeply is a heart that has been broken before. The love of one who has never experienced pain or loss will feel shallow and superficial. It is simply how it works here. We learn as much through our failures as we do from our successes... and sometimes more! No one develops strength, resilience, courage, compassion and endurance by having an easy, lazy, comfortable little life. Challenge is what stretches us to grow, and joy is a momentary reward until the next cycle of learning.

The myth of everlasting happiness is probably one of the greatest lies ever told. What does that even mean? Can you imagine being on that constant high of being SOOO HAPPYYYY! It would be not only unsustainable and exhausting, but quickly become monotone. Without the contrast of the highs and lows of life, even forever happiness would end up being the same old-same old. Happiness can be like a drug to the ego, one to which we become habituated. New happiness that comes into our lives is a rush, but sooner or later we become used to it and that happiness becomes our new normal. Then we find we need more "new happy stuff" to get that same rush of new happiness again. This is the same dynamic as that driving drug addiction: the chasing of the same level of exhilaration and relief we experienced the first time it worked, but it will never be the first time again. In any case, nothing in life lasts forever. Everlasting happiness is this unrealistic dream that just keeps you chasing after something that can never last. It is the greatest wild goose chase ever perpetrated on unsuspecting humans.

The hills and valleys of life are part of the cycles of learning. The more we embrace the gifts that each of them brings, the more we expand our range of experience, stretch our hearts and strengthen the mettle of our character. While egoic happiness is the endless pit that demands more and gets you nowhere, the Soul experiences the most contentment and satisfaction when we overcome, grow from, and master the challenges of our lives. Following our highest calling and achieving that which is meaningful to our Soul is where true fulfilment and inner peace lie. Ultimately, the evolving young Master soul must achieve equanimity. Equanimity is not a flat line desert of feeling; it is a sense of constant, steady balance at one's core. The Master still experiences the many colours on the palette of life, and they welcome them all without judgment. All the while, they are not at the mercy of the highs and low, a victim to the phenomena of experience, or assigning undeserved meaning to it. This too shall pass... but in the meantime, we must experience and feel life fully, without being enslaved to the sensations it provides our lower bodies. It is, like most things on the spiritual path, a finely tuned balance.

We Should Not Balance Light and Dark In Ourselves

Definitely not if you wish to become truly enlightened and masterful!

The common new-age statement that we need to balance light and dark within ourselves is a distortion of the understanding that we must face and accept our darkness in order to heal and become whole. What we fear or judge, cannot be healed. What we avoid or deny cannot be faced. In order to evolve and become more masterful and enlightened, we must look our darkness in the eye, own and make our peace with the choices and attitudes which have created this darkness, in order to then heal and process it out. Darkness is not your true nature, it is something that was created through making choices to go into separation from Spirit and form the light. Darkness is not a thing in itself, it is simply the absence of light.

Think for a minute on everything we have learnt so far about the process of initiation, the continuous refinement of our vibration, the purification of the lower bodies, the refinement of our character and the purification of the human vessel so that Spirit descend. Remember also that grounding more of our greater spiritual presence, and Spirit therefore merging with matter, produces spiritual light. The darkness within us is the part of us which exists in separation from the light and love of our Soul Tree. It is dark because the sun of spirit does not shine there anymore; it is the absence of spiritual light. It is the part of us that has turned away from God, locked in pain, resentment, shame or anger. It is the part of us where we have rejected love and enlightenment and gone into separation from Mother-Father God. We then usually judge and push away that part of us because it is painful, or not acceptable to others. This judgment and denial creates even more separation, including from ourselves. Most people are scared of the pain and personal demons which reside in these "dark" parts of us, but remember that we created these demons through holding on to our pain and judging it. Yes, we must break down the walls of denial, fear and judgment which separate us from darkness... in order to heal, enlighten and release it! Not to keep it there in its tortured, unresolved state. Balancing light and dark within ourselves basically means we must have as much darkness as we have light, or to allow only as much enlightenment to occur as there is darkness in us. It means getting stuck in our evolution because we refuse to enlighten our darkness. This makes no sense within the context of continuous spiritual evolution!

Our internal fear and darkness must, in divine timing and when we are ready, be faced, felt, acknowledge and accepted. We cannot fear it, we cannot judge it, but we must also not protect it, become identified with it or defend it. We must own our part in creating our inner monsters, and decide to relinquish them in favour of more love, more light and more spiritual truth. This is the only way to progress on the path of initiation. We always have a choice between love and fear. The unresolved darkness within us must be resolved and relinquished from a place of personal responsibility and acceptance. We must return all that we are and have been to love, to light and to God and Goddess. No part of us should be left behind, hiding in fear.

I will add as a side comment that there is also another aspect of existence often describes as "darkness", which the Void, also sometimes referred to as the Womb of the Goddess. This is a different sorts of "darkness". This dark Void, is not evil, wounded or about fear. It is simply the Void of the as-of-yet Uncreated. It is nothingness, black as night and empty of any created object, but also full of the potential energy of all that can be. The Void is nothing but can become anything and everything. It is the creative potential of our Universe. It is the liminal, the in-between of existence and non-existence. This is an expression of the Feminine aspect of Source, the receptive womb of the Universal Mother, waiting for the seed and spark of the Universal Father to co-create into Being. It is the void from which all is born and into which everything ends.

****

Spiritual Truth is always difficult to fathom, and even more difficult to convey in language. Words are always limiting, and spiritual revelations can never be adequately translated for those who have not had the direct experience of them. This makes spiritual truth particularly prone to misunderstanding, misinterpretation and distortion by those who may read or hear the words, but never had the profound, direct realisation of it themselves. In this chapter, I have attempted to convey the wisdom from my current levels of Knowing, particularly pertaining to topics I feel are too often spouted out like spiritual slogans, and oftentimes lacking the substance of personal integrated experience to back them.

The spiritual path does involve a certain amount of faking it until we make it. Everyone starts out needing to learn and practice what they do not know, from a teacher who has actually attained to and actualised the wisdom they teach. This means that everyone start out needing to take things on good faith, for a little while at least. After all, we don't know what we don't know. Yet even then, I encourage you to practice discernment in the Knowing of the heart and Soul. If nothing feels "off" against the compass of our deeper hearts, then we must be willing to give the unknown and the uncertain a go, trying on new concepts and understanding. A teacher must prove themselves to be someone you can trust to guide you through this process. This is how we try things on, explore new states and realities, shaping ourselves to their truth, until we finally click into place, have our own realisation of it, and become one with the Knowing of what we were taught. This is when our knowledge becomes our own, realised through us in its essence. But we have to start somewhere, and a good teacher can help us with this.

It is easy, in the exploratory phase of spiritual study, to think that understanding something in our mind, as an intellectual and conceptual necessity, is the same as truly getting it in spiritual terms. Genuine revelation and integration of new knowing means having that "Ah ha" experience of a new reality dawning upon us. We become one with it and it becomes a part of us. It is a transformation and multi-dimensional experience. Our thinker cannot possibly attain to the same depth and nuance of understanding as the one that comes with genuine spiritual realisation. Beware of this trap of confusing information stored in your thinker with true spiritual revelation. All the mind can grasp is like a reductive photocopy of the original Knowing. This is the problem with followers of the great teachers repeating the original teaching without having realised them in their own right. Over time, it creates distorted interpretation. The only remedy is for the followers themselves to attain to the same levels of realisation and actualisation. Learning new information and receiving spiritual teachings remains useful in opening the doors of our mind to a more vast experience of life. Faking it until we make it allows us to practice more masterful and enlightened ways of being. But it is the direct transmission of Gnosis, Knowing, where the true magic lies. Allow yourself to expand into and be with what your Soul Tree knows, and be willing to take instruction from great Souls, through the direct transmission of Gnosis. It always starts out with being as the child, as if knowing nothing and greeting everything anew, yet remaining anchored in the wise discernment of our spiritual heart.

CHAPTER 6

Where Do I Start?

~~~

It is all very well to explore the main lines of how Creation came to be, the structure of the Soul Tree, the process of initiation and address all these spiritual misconceptions... but what do we do with all this knowledge? How do we put these understandings into practice? Life is, after all, about grounding and expressing Love. A lot of knowledge is useless unless it helps us evolve, be of service, and live in more love and enlightenment. So how do we set our feet seriously on this road towards unified identification with our Soul Tree? And how do we undertake the serious work of spiritualisation and transformation on the path of Spiritual Alchemy and self-mastery?

As I shared in Chapter 1, the beginner Soul aspiring to the early stages of initiation is often better off embracing the path of Religion, for a time at least. Remember that the journey of initiation spans many lifetimes and we may not, in this life, need to journey the path of Saviourship if we have already progressed that way in previous embodiments, and retraced the steps of previous Soul attainment in this life. The Soul energy which animates and informs us in this life may have spent many lifetimes progressing on the Path of Religion. In this life, you may choose to continue on the Religious Path, or you may feel called to embark on a new phase of the journey by embracing the Path of Personal Spiritual Alchemy.

I will expand a little more about the path of Transformation through Mastery, and provide you with some practical tips on how to establish some foundational practices to get you started. Remember, however, that no one can, and no one has ever, achieved high levels of spiritual mastery or enlightenment alone. If you have not yet, you will eventually need to find your tribe and your teacher. I invite you to be discerning in this matter, to follow your wisdom and your heart's knowing as you allow your Soul Tree to guide you to the appropriate Teacher(s). Remember the three early tests on the path? Recognition, discernment and boundaries (See chapter 3). Feeling "energy" emanating from someone or their work is not enough. Energy can be many things, at all levels of vibration. A lot of astral plane energy can bamboozle us with glamour which brings relief to the personality, makes the ego feel empowered and special, but does not foster the Soul's growth. A lot of power, without love and light, can feel strong, but this is not what you want either. There is nothing wrong with power, but in order to function in harmony with our Universe, power must be put in the service of Love and Light, so that the Soul becomes powerfully loving. Be aware that the presence of power by itself in a teacher, without love and light, is not usually a good sign as it means they are on the dark path (regardless of what they claim). This world, however, needs less of the soppy, flabby lovey-dovey stuff and more of the powerfully loving stuff; so we need powerfully loving teachers and initiates, rather than fluffy ones. Yet, power alone, for its own sake, is destructive.

Choose a Teacher from whom you can feel a higher vibration of love and enlightenment, and, importantly, choose a Teacher whose professional, personal and spiritual ethics are very high indeed. A proper teacher must walk the talk of what they teach. Watch the false prophets that promise mastery or galactic activation in a handful of workshops. They may be well intentioned, but that does not mean they don't have egoic lack of clarity and glamour at play to make such unrealistic promises. No one is perfect, but a good Teacher will demonstrate a generous number of Mastery qualities. Be discerning but not obsessively fault finding, and be honest with yourself about whether it is your ego or your Soul which is attracted to a particular path and teacher. If you are present and connected to your Soul Tree, there will be a sense of recognition echoing from deep within your Soul to indicate that a Teacher is right for you at this stage in your growth, and perhaps in the long term.

The Path of Personal Spiritual Alchemy

As I shared in chapter 1, one of the main difference between the Path of Religion and the Path of Personal Spiritual Alchemy is the absence of an intermediary or Saviour to do some of the work for you, particularly the work of removing karmic impediments to your progression. The other major difference is that the Path of Saviourship relies on the mechanism of devotion to a Guru, Messiah, Prophet or Teacher. He provides an idealised human expression on which to model ourselves, and represents a pathway through which progression is facilitated, through His intercession. Followers adhere to moral values, rules of life and a set of practices in order to reinforce the moral growth and self-improving influence of the Teachings. The Path of Saviourship is overseen and energetically facilitated by the Planetary Spiritual Hierarchy, also known as The White Lodge, or the White Brotherhood. This is the inner plane organisation comprised of all the disciples, initiates and Masters who are on the path of love and light, and who are on the spiritual and ascension Path. Some of the beings which form the White Lodge are incarnate, but many are not. The Spiritual Hierarchy has existed on this planet for many thousands of year, and has helped provide pathways for the spiritual evolution of humanity through the Saviourship model.

The Path of Personal Spiritual Alchemy works in collaboration with the Planetary Hierarchy, but runs as a parallel stream of initiation overseen and supported by a group-memory consciousness called The Circle of Sirius. The Circle of Sirius is composed of a wide range of highly evolved beings from this world and many others throughout the Universe, including beings from other streams of evolution such as Guardian energies (who belong to the stream of Elementals/Angelics). These beings hold very high standards of purity and clarity, and have banded together to pool and share of their collective Knowing, in order to support the evolution and harmonising of worlds. The most advanced levels of this group-consciousness collective are at a point in their evolution when they are almost ready to transcend form existence altogether, and move into the formless realms of pure energy which is beyond anything we understand. They hope to pass on everything they know to assist evolving Souls who are behind them in the evolutionary chain, so that the whole system can learn from their experience and evolve. Planet Earth is at the very beginning of its most evolved Souls able to meet the criteria for entry into this group, but they seek to generously share their wisdom and assist the evolution of those who are ready and receptive.

On the Path of Alchemy, students are devoted to the God within and to our direct connection to the God above, which includes our direct connection to our Soul

Tree. Although we have Teachers, Guides and Mentors, there is no reliance on devotion to an external teacher or Messiah. The mechanism facilitating spiritual advancement is that of insight into personal and universal truth. Through their own practice and the support of their Teachers and Mentors, disciples face realisations, insights and epiphanies about themselves–including and especially the uncomfortable truths–and gradually earn their right to get a peek into the workings of Life and the Universe. Students must then undertake the work of removing, dissolving and transcending the things, within themselves, and in their lives, which are standing in the way of grounding and actualising the new wisdom. Certain balanced states of beings, attitudes, tools and techniques are learnt and mastered, so that the disciple may themselves carry out the clearing, transmuting, transforming and dissolving of the things holding them back. The students practice new masterful behaviours, new enlightened and wise attitudes and new alignments to spiritualised ideals. The thick of the work is a combination of transmuting and dissolving the old self-imposed limitations while also practicing new behaviours and realigning to higher ideals. This work is the fuel to the alchemical process of personal and spiritual transformation, but the magic of the transformation itself relies on many fine points of balance in our state of being, in partnership with our Soul Tree. The details of how this wondrous, transformative alchemical magic occurs cannot fully be explained or grasped by our monkey minds, and it can take time to master properly. Our thinker is not, and cannot be, what drives this process. The conscious mind's bad habit of wanting to know and control everything just ends up getting in the way. The teachings and mechanics must be studied and integrated, only to be turned into something altogether more than just understanding. It is essentially about entering a different, new and transformational state of being, in partnership with our Soul Tree. It is a journey of progression: the more we grow on the path of Alchemy, the more it becomes about being the transformer, rather than doing the transformation.

This is the path of Transformation through Mastery, and there is indeed a huge emphasis on the act of developing Mastery, across-the-board, in a balanced and integrated way. This includes becoming a Master of self at every level of the Self (higher and lower). The learning also involves mastery of our effect upon the world and our sphere of influence, as well as the mastery of the skills and abilities necessary to be of Service to the Divine Plan.

Everyone starts with psychological and emotional clarity. This is a non-negotiable aspect of the Alchemical Path. Without psychological and emotional clarity, the fear-based ego and its patterns can too easily highjack and short-circuit our best efforts and intentions, and distort the spiritual energy and information we receive. All energy coming from a Higher level to be channelled and grounded into the Earth plane has to come through the lower bodies. If our lower bodies are full of fear, pain, anger, shame, unworthiness, pre-conceived crystallised beliefs, rigid dogma and unconscious emotional patterns, then all the energy or Knowing coming through will be tainted by our unresolved issues. If you pour the purest and cleanest water through a dirty, muddy pipe, the water will always come out at the other end dirty regardless of how clear it started out. The same laws apply to the pure energy of Spirit coming through us. No matter how much we meditate, how expanded our consciousness becomes through the application of certain spiritual practices, unless we do the work of psychological and emotional clearing, we won't be able to ground and actualise it on the Earth plane with any real clarity or reliability. Sadly, the Earth plane is where the love and the light are most needed! This planet is struggling, and it is the job of every lightworker embodied in form to access higher vibrations of love and enlightened Knowing, in order to express it here, to ground it and make it take root in the world where it is so desperately needed. Without purification of our psyche, emotions and body, it is impossible to do so because our unresolved fear will filter and distort what we bring in.

The path of Transformation through Mastery is one of self meeting Self, at every level of our being, time and time again. It can be a most profoundly beautiful and humbling process, and also a most confronting and harrowing one. It is not for everyone. It requires a certain amount of courage, confront, strength of will and the willingness to be humbled, to be wrong, to be wrong again, to let go of everything and start again without knowing how to. Some like the idea of the Alchemical path based on wizard-like fantasies, the glamour of doing magic, knowing secret symbols and quoting ancient mysteries, but they struggle with the long-term commitment to the work of psychological clarity. Those who seek a less confronting path are usually better suited to the Path of Saviourship.

The concept of integration is another key aspect of this path. To be integrated means to have an integrated mind, body, Soul and spirit. This means that the Spirit Forest, the Soul Tree, the individual Soul and the body-mind all work together in an interconnected and collaborative manner. All levels of the lower and of the Higher Self work together as a team, each playing their part in service to the Higher Love. The soul has control of the body-mind, and is in turn fully dedicated to serving the Higher Self and the Divine Plan. Through the achievement of self-mastery and the surrendering to being guided, informed and inhabited by our Soul Tree and Monad, we become a seamless channel and clear service vessel for Divine Will, Divine Love and Wisdom, and Spiritual Intelligence. We become indeed a living Source of Love, Light and Divine Truth on the planet, to the planet and for the planet. Much of what is the separate, fear-based egoic self has to be gradually dissolved and surrendered so we become the empty vessel waiting to be filled with Spirit, or in other words, by the energy and presence of our Soul Tree and Monad, our True Self. The Alchemical Path involves the progressive development of a profound mystical and occult relationship with almost everything: ourselves, the timeline of our Soul journey through eternity, with Love itself, with Life itself and with Source on every level of existence. The disciple's energy and consciousness purifies and expands into the Mind of God, and everything comes alive. Reality is never the same, but it all starts with the student being willing to embrace radical change, confront their bullshit and transform everything they are and know in surrender to the larger Being that they are a part of.

As the initiate Soul undertakes the continuous work of clearing self-imposed limitations from their body-mind, they also purify and clear out the energy they have set in motion through time, in this life and in the many incarnations of the Soul. This is the karmic clearing part of the process. We start by clearing and harmonising our individual karmic mess as an embodiment, in this life. But as we complete Soul merge, we begin the clearing of our Soul karma through the timeline on this planet. As we continue to grow and integrate with more of the energy of our Soul Tree, the karmic clearing process continues to the Soul Group level, and to Oversoul level, and to Monadic level. Every initiate who takes the higher planetary initiations must purify and refine their planetary karmic balance in order to progress and eventually complete planetary Ascension. Our planetary karmic balance is the accumulated total energy of our effect on the world over the entire re-incarnational journey of our Soul (and Soul Tree) on this planet, through all of time. Remember that from the perspective of the Oversoul and Monad, points along the timeline are not separate, but a unified time field and flow. The energy that we, as Souls, set in motion and radiate into the world through our words, thoughts, actions, projections and choices are our creation and our karmic responsibility. Our influence, outputs and creations are an energetic extension of us and form part of what is called our environmental body, or our sphere of influence. This influential sphere extends in space, across everything which is part of our lives and everything we are connected to, but also through time along the flow of our Soul's journey. Any energy which we put out or set in motion, and which is unresolved or not refined enough in vibration, must be purified and spiritualised too. This connects to the process of Soul and Monadic braiding mentioned in previous chapters. The Path of Personal Spiritual Alchemy allows us to do this for ourselves, in our own right, thereby enabling our own progression through the initiation process. Please bear in mind that this is a progressive journey; it takes time for the student to learn how to do all of this effectively and without wavering from their steadiness in love and light. It may sound simple, but it is not easy. This is why a teacher is crucial, as they will support, inspire, mentor, teach, protect and help facilitate the student's journey, while challenging and gradually helping the student to stand on their own two feet in every aspect of Mastery.

Not even the greatest Spiritual Masters can possibly know everything or be proficient at everything. Masters on the Path of Alchemy have, however, answered the call from their Soul Tree, taken ownership of their growth and God realisation process, and mastered every aspect of learning necessary to fulfil their service purpose in the Divine Plan. The truly great Masters like to gain a wide base of learning, and try to have basic working knowledge in many areas of human endeavour.

The mastering of all the necessary skills, tools, attunement, alignments and states of being cannot be taught in a book. It takes years of diligent study and practice, which then turns into lifetimes within the context of our eternal evolution. The ancient mystery schools functioned this way: neophyte students often entered the mystery schools at a young age to spend the rest of their lives training. When they died, it was not unusual to reincarnate and do it all over again to keep progressing! Times have changed, and the world is now the mystery school at large, but the training is still something which takes long term dedication and practice. It is the ancient way; it is the way. Imagine telling the ancient mystery school Masters about people completing their curriculum of spiritual transformation in a few workshops, or even a few years of study... They would have laughed and claimed it a joke! The journey of initiation and evolution is more extensive than the little ego can even comprehend. It is an eternal journey. In many ways, it never ends because once someone has completed planetary ascension, they begin their solar initiation process, and then we move on to the galactic initiations, and then to the Universal level, and so on. No matter how advanced the Soul is, we constantly discover new horizons beyond what we know and have experienced. We must learn to embrace the wonder of the journey in itself, instead of obsessing with the attainment of a fixed destination. Evolution is an eternal spiral. Cycles repeat, expand out and flow into the next; Life continues on and on. We are part of this dance of

Life. Relinquish the need for certainty and static goals. Grow comfortable with the notions of exploring eternity and infinity. The right life attitude will help you more joyfully navigate this great evolutionary adventure we are all on.

Where do I start? A Few Basics to Get Things Flowing

Regardless of where you are at in your quest to find a teacher (or school) to support your alchemical journey, there are practices, alignments and habits which you can implement immediately to get you on your way. The following tips will help you to kickstart the journey of developing a relationship with your Soul Tree, to establish a foundational basis for psychological and emotional clearing, and to realign towards living in harmony with the natural order of our Universe.

- Start Daily Spiritual Practices

In order to be successful on the spiritual path, your spirituality must become one of the very most important things in your life. Like everything which is very important, you must dedicate time and energy to it every single day. The things you do not consistently tend to will wither and die; the things you nurture will grow and thrive.

We all have a daily routine: We get up, shower, brush our teeth, have breakfast, exercise and go to work. Maybe we also have a routine at work: The tasks we perform, what order we perform them in, meetings we routinely attend and the steps to get the job done each day and each week. Our evening routine may include exercise, picking up the kids from school, cooking family dinner, spending some time with our partner, reading before bed and so on. We have trained ourselves into these routines because they help ensure we do everything we need to do in a day, or in a week: Tend to our hygiene, look after our health, make time to nurture the important relationships in our life, earn a living and do good work. In the same way, progress and success on the spiritual path can only occur if you set in place a routine which ensures that your spiritual growth is nourished and strengthened every day of your life. A once-a-week meditation practice or personal growth class will never be enough for notable success. Such part-time commitment is what we call recreational spirituality: it's like a side hobby, not a serious commitment. It's nice, it's fun, it's better than nothing…but it bears only marginal, slow growth. A musician committed to mastering their instrument must practice every day—not once a week - or they will never play well. Spiritual progression and the achievement of Self-Mastery is the same. There are many hours in a day and even more in a week. If you are not engaging with a spiritual focus, topic or practice for a goodly portion of your time, then the clunky egoic world of third-dimensional existence is going to drown out the voice of Spirit in your life. There is much temptation, darkness, noise, distraction, laziness, hedonism and heaviness in the world, which will be a force of inertia opposing your evolution. Regular spiritual clearing, practice and focus will be key in offsetting this collective egoic inertia, as well as the resistance of your own negative ego. You then need to invest a little extra effort in order to do more than just offset the inertia, and actually move forward with your growth.

A daily morning spiritual routine can do wonders to get you into a space of more flow, clarity, peace and a more centred connection to yourself and your Soul Tree, as you prepare to face the world. A spiritual practice routine in the evening is great to help you land from your day, come back to centre, reflect on the experiences and challenges you may have had, integrate your learning, clear any unresolved issues, as well as wind down before bed. Feeling too tired to do your nightly practices? Actually, being tired is a great time to do some self-reflection and soul searching as the negative ego will be low on energy, and less likely to resist and get in the way. Remember, discipline requires the use of your will. Just like you must push through your laziness and resistance to go to the gym to look after your physical health and fitness, so you must use your will to push through your egoic laziness and resistance to doing your daily spiritual practices consistently, no matter what!

I started independently creating my own routine of daily spiritual practices in my early twenties, based on a collection of teaching points and practices gathered from my spiritual reading and various classes. I carried out my practices daily, even very late at night after long shifts at work, for a couple of years before I encountered my spiritual tribe. I intuitively knew and felt that a disciplined approach was going to be the only way to make consistent progress. I also knew enough of the long-standing spiritual traditions of our world to realise they all insisted on their students following a regime of daily disciplines. I have included below some practices which I consider key for the aspiring alchemical student.

- Protect, Align and Clear You Energy System Everyday

Cleanliness is godliness! One of the most important daily practices for someone on the spiritual path is that of energetic hygiene and protection. Every day, we take care of our physical hygiene by cleaning our physical bodies. But our physical bodies are not the only ones which accumulate dirt, debris and other unpleasant matter. Every day, as we move through the world, we produce or collect energy that can end up sitting in our energy field. The type of energy accumulated in our field depends on the energetic clarity of the spaces we hang out in, the people we surround ourselves with, the strength of our boundaries and the quality of our own thoughts, emotions and reactions.

Other people's thoughts, opinions and emotions may get energetically projected towards us and into our field. If we have poor energetic boundaries, being close to others who carry a lot of fear, negative energy, or denied emotion can affect our vibration. If we walk around without proper protection, we can collect etheric, astral or mental debris that were left dumped around the place by other people. Our own internal experience and activity will leave energetic debris and smears in our four-body system. Half-finished thought forms or emotional residue can linger in our mental and astral bodies and slowly rot (yes, forms on the various planes of existence can grow, die and rot like they do on the physical plane). To support the purification and raising our vibration, we must protect ourselves from being overly affected by the negativity around us. We must also clear, on a daily basis, the remnants of energetic activity and interactions, or those picked up from our environment. We recommend a twice-a-day clearing: one first thing in the morning, and again before going to bed at night. The morning clearing is a great way to start the day: clear out any residues from our nightly processes, dreams and potential energetic interactions in the sleep-state, get clear, and set our alignment for the day. The evening clearing is important to clear out the muck from the day and go to sleep clean and clear. Energetic hygiene can be repeated anytime throughout the day, as you feel the need to. Just remember, like anything on the spiritual path, you must approach this in love, not fear. Protection, boundaries and clearing can't be an act of spiritual paranoia; it must be about self-love and self-care.

How do you clear your energy? Through certain physical and meditative practices, done with feeling and accompanied by visualisation and intent. Do not underestimate the impact of intention, visualisation, and using our own energy through feeling, all of which are the basis of any spiritual work.

SETTLE DOWN

In order to do your daily energy hygiene routine, make sure you are in a settled space within yourself: grounded, centred and present in the moment. If you need to, take a few deep, slow breaths. Release tension, distraction or stress on the out-breath, and use the in-breath and centre your energy into your heart chakra. Do this until you feel you have slowed down and are in the moment, present in your body. No one can get themselves into a clear space when scattered and agitated. So the first thing is to settle down and be here now.

GET CENTRED

Make sure you connect with the energetic space at the centre of your chest, where your heart chakra is. The heart space is the energetic centre of your lower vehicles and should be where your presence is centrally focused and radiating out. Intend and visualise your heart centre as your central Sun, and feel your energy centering there. Feel anchored in your heart centre, present with yourself.

GROUND

You must also be grounded in your physical body and connected with the Earth Mother. This is an important part of being present: Feel your energy grounded properly, all the way into and throughout your physical body. Inhabit the entirety of your physical body with your presence, and then also feel your connection with the Earth and into the Earth, through your feet. Remember, we are a part of Gaia and we are connected with her through our grounding cord, which anchors our energy into the Earth like a root of energy.

PROTECTION AND BOUNDARIES

The first thing to put into place is protection and correct energetic boundaries. If your energy field is protected and you hold strong self-loving boundaries, fewer negative energies are going to enter your field or affect you. An easy and common protection technique is that of visualising and feeling a strong, bright bubble of golden light surround your entire energetic field, or aura. You soul vehicle, your mind, your emotional body and your physical body must all be held within this big, strong, bright bubble. Know, intend and feel this bubble to be an impenetrable shield of light, blocking and repelling all negativity. Please be aware that energetic protection of love only works if you yourself are not actively engaging in fear. The golden bubble will protect love from fear. As long as you maintain your own energy in the bandwidth of love, you will be protected. As soon as you engage in activities of fear, attack or judgment, the protection of your bubble will be negated as you yourself have filled your own field with fear. If this happens, catch yourself, stop, breathe, own your fear, choose otherwise, let it go and reassert your golden bubble of protection.

Holding better personal boundaries will be the other side of protecting your energy from negativity. This is as much an attitude as it is a way to hold space for yourself. Make your golden bubble and energy field stronger by intending to hold a clear, strong space of love and light within your bubble. Affirm, mentally and verbally, with intent, that you accept and express only vibrations of unconditional love and above into your field. Learn to say no to that which does not feel right. Learn to ignore those who seek to goad you into conflict or fear. Learn to respect yourself and hold your own energy in respect and clarity, while remaining in humility. Do not let other people drag you down or suck your energy, and do not do this to them either. Boundaries, like protection, also work both ways. If you do not respect yourself, others are not likely to respect you. Likewise, if you do not respect other people's boundaries, your own boundaries will be weakened and others are less likely to treat you with respect. The process of effectively setting healthy, clear and wise boundaries improves as you grow, because the quality of your boundaries is a function of your level of self-love, respect for self and others, and of wisdom and discernment. The more masterful and wise you become, the stronger your boundaries of love will be.

CLEAR YOUR ENERGY

Once protection and boundaries are in place, we go about clearing the negativity or energetic debris present in your field. There are physical and energetic approaches which can assist with energetic clearing.

It should come as no surprise that water can be useful in cleansing, particularly on the physical, etheric and astral levels of the self. Adding intent and visualisation can make this more effective. Be present, centred and grounded as described in previous paragraphs, and extend your energy to connect up towards your Soul Tree, extending your energy like a column of light rising through the top of your head. Use this upward connection to call in a down-pouring of white spiritual light from your Higher Self. Standing in the shower, visualise, feel and intend the water to blend with the white light pouring through your field. Feel and know the water and the white light to be one, as you allow them to clear your energy as it runs through. Be grateful to the Spirit of the element of water for this assistance. Swimming in water, particularly salt water, can also be very cleansing as salt is a purifying substance. This is why swimming in the ocean can be so purifying and rejuvenating! Having baths with Epsom salts and sea salt (preferably one free of chemical or anti-caking additive) is a helpful practice to clear and rebalance body and energy. As you make use of water for its energetic cleansing properties, it is always very important that you be grateful for the water and to the element of water, as you release into the water whatever needs to be cleansed away. The gratitude will help bring some positive energy into the water that collected your debris, which will be helpful as the water returns to Mother Earth. The water is doing you a service, and it is important to appreciate this as it returns to Gaia.

Other practices such as smudging, the use of incense or fire smoke can be helpful to a degree, though the effectiveness depends on the quality of the herbs used and the clear intent of the person using them. Being near an open fire for some time, and allowing the energy of the fire and its etheric glow to burn and consume any of the dross in your energy is another useful way to use the elements for cleansing. Again, approach this with gratitude for the fire, and to the fire.

Remember that only that which you allow to be released can be cleared! If you hold on to energy or judge it, it will stay right in your field. Be aware also that letting go is not the same as pushing away. Just allow, be in acceptance, open and whatever does not belong in your field can be cleared and cleansed.

Another most potent tool for clearing, refining and transmuting energy is the Violet Flame.

The Cosmosis® Mentoring Centre has a great free introductory course on Energetic Hygiene, which teaches you to access a more detailed routine for clearing your energy. See our details in the next chapter.

- Work with The Violet Flame

The Violet Flame is a potent helper to clear your energy field, raise your vibration, and support personal transformation. I strongly recommend you use it daily, and it is very easy to include the Violet Flame as part of your daily energetic hygiene routine. The Violet Flame is an aspect of one of the Divine Ray energies. I am referring to the Cosmic rays, which are expressions of Unified Source Energy after it subdivided into grand streams of defining qualities. You know how a rainbow, or a prism, reveal the seven colours of the light spectrum? These colours are an earthly manifestation of the Rays, which are all aspects of the One Light of Source. The Violet Flame is one aspect of the Seventh Ray, or the violet ray. This is a powerful energy of transformation, refinement and purification. It raises the vibration of any energy which is bathed in it, and helps transmute negativity and fear into vibrations of unconditional love and above. This energy plays a key role in the Age of Aquarius and all those who walk the spiritual path are encouraged to work with it.

As part of your daily energetic hygiene routine, get yourself into a settled, centred and grounded space, surrounded by your golden bubble of protection. Take a few deep, slow breaths and focus on being fully present, deeply connected into your heart-centre in the middle of your chest, and grounded into the Earth.

Connect with your heart and connect upwards by extending your energy from the heart and up through your crown connection at the top of your head, towards your Soul Tree. Then, either silently or out loud (as you prefer), call in for a down-pouring and deep penetration of the Violet Flame, throughout your entire energy field and four-body system, and then through you into the Earth. Visualise a shower of violet fire pouring down, going into every cell and nook and cranny of your physical, emotional, mental and Buddhic vehicles. Allow each of your chakras to be deeply bathed in this violet fire for a little while, as you allow and release into the flame all that no longer serves you, with acceptance and gratitude. Allow yourself to open and dissolve all that no longer serves your evolution, and to raise your vibration. As it continues to actively flow and burn away the dross in your field, allow it to flow into the Earth, with gratitude, as you respectfully share this energy with Gaia, our Earth Mother. When you feel that you are finished, express gratitude to the energy of the Violet Flame, take a deep breath. Make sure you are properly grounded here now, and open your eyes.

If you wish to experiment a little more with another Violet Flame meditation, the Cosmosis® Mentoring Centre has a Planetary Healing Violet Flame meditation available on our YouTube channel. Go to the Cosmosis® Mentoring Centre channel and search for a video called "Working with the Violet Flame" (it is in the Spiritual Alchemy playlist).

- Meditation and Prayer

All spiritual traditions, whether religious or alchemical, western or eastern, make use of daily meditation and prayer. But what is the difference?

In the simplest of terms, we could say that prayer is talking to God and mediation is listening to God. Both are closely related, like two sides of the same coin.

Prayer is often misunderstood. Many people seem to confuse God with Santa Claus as it's not uncommon to see people approach prayer like a well-meaning Christmas wish list: "Hi God, I've been good today, so I'd like for Mary to find a man who loves her, and I'd like to have the money to buy a new car. Oh! And please make grandma well again. Thanks God!" While it is understandable that people in need turn to God for answers to their problems, this Santa Claus approach to prayer is, from the perspective of the Spiritual Masters, an immature way to do it. It is like adult children who, after leaving the nest of their parent's home, only call or visit when they want something. It's just not endearing and reveals a certain amount of self-centeredness. The masterful way of talking to God is not about asking for stuff your ego wants. Proper prayers is about asking God for guidance about two key things:

- Please help me learn and grow in order to become the best version of myself possible, so that I can serve to my greatest capacity. Guide me to the experiences and realisations I need to do so. Amen.

- Hi God, or Universe, or Soul Tree. How may I be of service today?

The role of prayer is for you, as the little embodied leaf, to make the effort to extend towards your Soul Tree and make contact. It shows that you are interested. In response, the Soul Tree may, in time, extend towards you. The Soul Tree, or the Universe, is not interested in a relationship which is about you asking for stuff all the time, and giving very little in exchange which is of evolutionary value. The Soul Tree is interested in evolving. Your prayers must be in support of your Soul Tree's interest, in service to All That Is. Prayer is about developing a relationship with your Soul Tree, and beyond, so that you may partner together to help you evolve, be of service to the greater Being that you are a part of and perhaps be of service to the world.

Meditation, on the other hand, is about learning to be still so you can hear the whispers and guidance of God, or in other words your Soul Tree. Meditation can take years to master because many people live in a constantly agitated state: stressed, busy with mind chatter, plagued with unruly emotions and unintentional thoughts. Most people are comfortable with doing stuff, but not very good at just being. The ability to still our mind and still our emotions is the main skill to be learnt when we learn to meditate. Only when we are still, deeply connected into our hearts and connected up to our Tree, may we be able to hear the voice of Spirit. To learn to feel one's feelings rather than keeping them bottled up can go a long way towards stilling an agitated emotional or mental body. Beyond that, it is discipline and consistent practice which will help you master the monkey into stillness and receptivity.

There are many simple meditation techniques out there, many of them involving breathing, mindfully experiencing the moment through your senses (without thinking about it) and noting one's thoughts as you allow them to pass and be released. Some meditation techniques are designed to help you become still and enter a slow brain-wave state, which helps release stress and regenerate. Such methods can easily be found through many meditation apps, and in books for the beginner meditator. Some meditations involve releasing tension from the body, while others include visualisation and specific spiritual focuses. Other meditations, aimed at the meditator who is already able to still their minds and enter an altered meditative state, are designed to expand your consciousness and commune with higher energies and the energy of your Soul Tree, in order to receive insight or guidance. Once we enter an altered meditative state, we can commune with an array of energies and beings, on higher planes or within nature. The capacity to go into a meditative state is the doorway through which spiritual communication and communion can occur. As always and even when meditating, we must maintain our protection, boundaries of unconditional love and discernment. If you meditate to commune with spiritual beings and energies, make sure that you have these precautions in place and always intend clearly to communicate only with beings of love, light and truth from the higher mental plane and beyond, in service of your highest good and the highest good of All That Is. Nothing less. Mother-Father God, Thy Will, not my will, be done.

Please see the resource at the end of this chapter for an easy daily meditation for energy clearing, working with the violet flame, and to align and connect to your Soul Tree.

- Grow Roots and Build your Antahkarana Bridge

The Antahkarana is the bridge of light which connects us to our Higher Self, through the crown chakra at the top of our head, and through the various levels of our mental bodies. It is the direct path of connection and communication between us as embodied leaves, and our Soul Tree and its Knowing. The development and strengthening of the Antahkarana Bridge goes hand in hand with progress through the initiations. It begins as the thin stretching of light filaments upwards towards the Soul, and then grows into a stronger connection and cord of light up until its full actualisation at the sixth initiation. It is important to put intention on connecting upwards to build and strengthen this connection to our Higher Self. This practice is easily included in our daily clearing and alignment meditation (see the meditation resource below) through the use of intent, visualisation and the choice to project tendrils or cord of our energy upwards through the top of our head, and all the way into the various levels of our Higher Self that we can connect with. When the Antahkarana bridge is well in place, it can be used for two-way energy exchange and energetic communication between you and your Higher Self, and help facilitate the descent of higher presence into the physical plane. You can extend upwards to pray in a masterful way, and you can be open and receptive to potential guidance or down-pouring of energy, if the Soul Tree deems it timely.

On the other extremity of our body, we also need to make sure that we ground our energy and presence into our body, and also into the earth. Slowing down, becoming very present in our body and feeling our connection with Mother Earth through our feet is a great way to do this. Visualise energetic roots, or one big solid grounding cord, coming out of your body through the soles of your feet, and going down deep into Gaia, and all the way into her heart and core. Being grounded is important because we must bring our love, light and spiritual presence here, into the world of matter, in order to spiritualise matter. This serves our own evolution and contributes to the spiritualisation of our planet.

- Self-Reflect, Journal and Review

Know Thyself! There were the famous words written at the entrance of the Temple of Delphi in ancient Greece, and indeed a common motto among ancient mystery schools. But why does it matter so much? And what does it really mean anyway?

First of all, as above, so below. Many things about life can be understood if we begin by truly understanding ourselves in a deep, honest and meaningful way. We are lower correspondences of a greater Whole, microcosm versions of the macrocosm. By observing, studying and knowing ourselves and the life which constantly unfolds within us physically, emotionally, mentally and spiritually, we may learn a lot about who and what we are, about how energy works, how interactions occur and about our place within the Universe.

Secondly, introspection is the only way to bring to the surface of our consciousness all aspects of our psyche, emotions and karmic influences. Human beings are a little bit like icebergs, in that the conscious part of us - the part we most identify with as we go about our daily lives -is but the tip of the iceberg of our whole being. Much of our behavioural programming, psychological patterning and emotional baggage hides behind a veneer of avoidance and denial because its origins are long forgotten, stored into the habit or instinctive minds, and the feelings are sometimes painful or shameful. Facing it all at once would be too much to handle while functioning in the world with sanity. The Universe is kind, so she tempers and times the uncovering of our hidden inner layers at a pace that we are ready for. When we have the psychological and emotional tools and resilience to confront the hidden layers within, the pace of the clearing can accelerate as we are now capable of dealing with that surfaces. It is Universal Law that we are never presented with anything we cannot handle. There is always a way. We may choose to embrace our readiness or shrink away in fear and overwhelmed, but we are, as a matter of fact, always capable of facing the feelings and challenges that life presents us with…otherwise they would not be presenting. We are often stronger than we think, yet it is always our choice to remember it.

Habits of self-reflection, soul searching and self-observation help us gently lift the veils of what is under the surface. We can't avoid the truth forever. Even when we think all the unwanted stuff is safely hidden away, it is always influencing us in ways that we may not be conscious of. These deeper feelings and deeper motives may reveals themselves if if we stop and look under the surface, if we ask ourselves pertinent questions with a genuine desire to know the truth. This is how we get ahead of our issues before they get on top of us. Such questions may include:

- What am I really feeling right now?

- How do I really feel about this, if I am honest with myself?

- What is important to me in these moments? or in life?

- Why am I doing what I am doing? Is this what I really choose for myself?

- What is driving my behaviour right now, if I am honest? What are my true motives?

- What needs am I trying to fulfil by engaging with this behaviour or activity? IS that healthy? Is it serving me?

- Where am I in my life's journey? Where am I going with it all? Are my daily choices and actions helping me get closer to my goals, or further from them?

- What are my values? What is my vision for life/work/my spiritual journey?

- Are my choices and actions reflecting my values and vision?

- What are my personal ethics? What do I consider okay and ethical? What don't I consider ethical and okay? What should I not tolerate in order to be true to my values and ethics?

Certain questions are more about reviewing your day or week, and learning from your experience in order to gain wisdom and improve your daily mastery:

- How did I do today, in terms of being masterful and loving?

- What reactions and triggers did I experience? How can I handle this better next time?

- Did I walk the talk of my values and goals? If not, why not?

- What was useful today and what was not?

- What gets in the way of me making better choices? What sabotages me?

- What could I do differently? How can I support myself and put strategies into place to help me do better?

Journaling can be helpful for many people as a way of exploring all these questions, but there are other ways.

Some people like to sit, perhaps with a cup of tea in a comfy chair, or somewhere in nature, and simply be with themselves as they ponder, feel and explore their innerness in silent questioning from the heart. Others work better while going for a quiet walk alone, like a sort of walking meditation, which keeps their body occupied while they soul search, review and wonder.

Remember, life is a school. We must go through life consciously, not like mindless zombies, if we are to learn from our experience and turn it into wisdom and mastery. Daily habits of soul searching, self-reflection and review are an absolutely central part of this path of Personal Spiritual Alchemy.

Another useful tip is to do a nightly review. A final review of your day just before bed at night helps cement the day's learning right before the integrative sleep process, when the psyche sorts out what to integrate and what to delete in the memory banks, and what to upload to Soul level as valuable learning. This is probably one of the best time of day to engage in self-review. But mini-reviews throughout the day, or whenever you have the space, can be helpful too as you reset and realign to your goals and values on the go.

-Take Responsibility and work with the Universal Mirror

This habit goes hand in hand with the self-reflection and review process. It is a very popular attitude these days to be a victim. Victim consciousness is a psychological epidemic: everyone wants to blame, sue or attack everyone else for their problems and their pain. This attitude of victimhood is completely contrary to what is good for our evolution and inner peace. Being a victim is a choice and ultimately an illusion. When we cast ourselves as victims, we become helpless and unable to change our destiny. We also cannot learn our lessons because we consider others to be at fault, and refuse to look in the mirror for our part of responsibility in the equation (even if that responsibility is how we respond to the situation). It will never, in the long term, lead to genuine healing, growth or wholeness of self. Bad things happen to everyone, but we always have a choice about what we do with it. No one is a victim, it's a fallacy.

Life unfolds according to the primary directive of the Divine Plan. We are here to learn, to grow and evolve. To this end, life works like a mirror: it reflects back to us our own internal landscape. The things that keep manifesting in our life, the consistent issues and problems we seem to run into, are not random. They are reflections of the energy we have been putting out over time, given back to us through the wonderful mechanism of the Universal Mirror. Remember, the Universe will always use our free will choices and energetic contributions, and use them to help us manifest the lessons we need to learn. If you don't like what you get, you need to change your input into the great Universal computer. Turning things around can take some time, especially if you have been living according to bad habits for lifetimes; but keep stepping towards love. Eventually, your karmic ship will turn around and your life will change. It all begins at the creative core of your experience: you.

We cannot control what other people think, do or choose. We cannot control life and we certainly cannot control God. We can only control what we do, what we choose and how we respond to life. Our attitude is our choice, our feeling responses and reactions are our choice. If you are a victim to your beliefs, your emotions or your physical urges, then you will feel like you do not have control over your body's desires, your emotional reactions and your thoughts. Soul will just be along for the ride and seek to blame the mirror of life for all your bad feelings. This is being an unconscious ego: blindly going through life reacting according to the psychological and emotional patterns we carry, a slave to both your body and your programming. There is no enlightenment, no mastery, and not even true agency living this way. The unconscious ego cannot see their unconsciousness, just like the sleeping person cannot see that they are sleeping. At some point, an awakening must happen where a new self-awareness reveals to us our shortcomings, our contribution to the outplay of our life, and the fact that we have a choice about changing how we go about it all. If we want different results, we need to do things differently!

The first step is to work on gaining self-control, and eventually gaining Soul control. We cannot do that without taking full responsibility for our part in the great work of life. No matter what happens to you or around you, no matter what others do or say, your reactions and your feelings are absolutely, always, without fail, YOUR choice and YOUR responsibility. Two people faced with the same difficulties may respond in a completely different manner, which just proves that there is no infallible equation of "event = response" in life. Our responses are always subjective, based on what we make things mean, what we assign importance to and whether certain events push the buttons of emotional triggers already present within us. We must own our subjective responses to life. Someone said something mean to you? It doesn't mean that you should be upset; why do you even care what they think? You had one traumatic accident? It does not mean that you should live in fear for the rest of your life. It is faulty cognition to draw general conclusions from an isolated event. Something which happened in the past does not have to define your future! Don't you want to champion yourself and rise again? Or are you going to let the abusers and attackers of the world win and keep you down?

Nothing that happens is reason enough to go into fear, or stay stuck there. It is normal and understandable to feel many upas and down as we go through the crazy ride of life; being alive means you'll always be feeling something. But we have a choice about which feelings we feed and hold on to, and which we let go of and dissolve. Regardless of the roller coaster of our experiences, how we get through it and get back up on our feet to fight another day is completely within our self-determining power to decide. There are attitudes, tools and practices that we can learn to do life more effectively; some of them are shared in this book. But the very first step is always to stop blaming, stop being a helpless victim, and take responsibility for our feelings and choices.

Bring everything you feel back to yourself and ask yourself: Is this a helpful way to respond? Why am I responding this way? What is this response showing me about myself? What are the underlying feelings and beliefs driving this? What do I need to address and let go of within myself in order to have healthier and more masterful responses? What new attitude or orientation is going to help me respond more wisely and masterfully? How can I train myself out of feeling like a victim, and into owning my destiny? Be aware that simply suppressing or denying what you feel, and your underlying issues, never works in the long run. Avoidance and denial only ends up causing more issues because our unfinished evolutionary business always seeks healing and completion. Everything has to come out at some point and Source works through us towards our evolutionary destiny. Better face it and release it than force it back down. If you find yourself facing big internal issues and feel overwhelmed, do seek help from a compassionate professional counsellor, therapist, mentor or coach (whichever is most relevant to your needs).

-Learn to Love the Truth and Confront the Uncomfortable

In order to take responsibility for what the mirror of life reflects to us of our own self and karma, you must have the balls to face the uncomfortable truths and our own uncomfortable feelings.

In the moments when the Soul Tree and the Universal Mirror seek to reveal your shortcomings or self-imposed limitations to you, the fearful ego will want to turn away, run scared, avoid, deny or blame the mirror. You know you're not perfect, right? Surely, you realise you are not at the pinnacle of evolutionary potential? Obviously, it means there is room for improvement. If you think you're there, you've got nowhere to go. If you think you're right all the time, you've got nothing to learn. And that's just the thing: You must be willing to be wrong, often. Life can mirror these things to you through manifesting the result of your choices. Choice/input leads to result/consequence. Don't attack the computer; look at the operator.

Situations where other people call you on your shortcomings can be more nuanced. I am not advising anyone to automatically take on board every criticism directed at you. Sometimes other people's attack are all about them and their reactions, and not much about you. Sometimes, it is a co-creation between two people who can improve their life input. Sometimes, however, it is mostly on you. Regardless of the situation, you should at least be willing to reflect honestly on the criticism you receive from others. Approach it in humility, with a desire for truth, and see if that other person may be a little bit right after all... or perhaps a lot. At best, you'll learn something about yourself; at worst, you'll learn something about them, or about life. In any case, you've learnt something, so you've got nothing to lose. Some people have a neurotic tendency to take responsibility for everything and assume they are at fault. Others do the opposite and always see fault in the other person, never themselves. Watch these unhealthy extremes and love the truth, no matter what it is.

If we wish to grow, become a brighter version of ourselves, and become a clear vessel for the Soul Tree's energy, there are two things we need to do:

- Remove all the traits, baggage and self-imposed limitations which are holding your back from returning to a state of grace as a clear expression of your Soul Tree. This is the process of unbecoming and unravelling the limiting layers that we, as Souls, have placed upon ourselves by making choices of fear or contraction. Much of the process of returning to our Spiritual Home and our true Selves is one of unbecoming, to reveal the essence within and make room for more of our greater spiritual Presence. It is often about doing less than doing more.

- Grow and reinforce spiritualised qualities and skills to nurture the expression of the great love, light, wisdom and intelligence of your Soul Tree through you. This is the re-training and personal development aspect: rounding out your mastery, and acquiring the skills and expertise necessary to be useful to the Tree, to the Planet and to Source.

The journey can be challenging, and it is one of self meeting Self time and time again. There will be stark reflections you must be willing to see. Remember, if you are emotionally charged, in judgment or have a reaction to anything someone says or does, then you have an issue to address. If anything the mirror of life reflects back at you upsets you or makes you drop into victim consciousness, then you have an issue to address. Those who have no issues don't get triggered, defensive or go into victim mode. This is always a good barometer of your state of clarity. Be grateful for the Universal mirror of life!

- Habits of Gratitude

Gratitude is an uplifting and transformative energy, and a key to partnering with the benevolence of the Universe. It can assist us to find the hidden gifts of life, foster a positive attitude, and attract abundance of the good stuff life has to offer. People generally demand a reason to be grateful: "Hey, listen God, if you want me to be grateful, then give me something to be grateful for!" This is completely upside-down and reveals a serious egoic entitlement. Do you think that you're so special, so important, that God has an obligation to make you happy? To make you feel good? To indulge all your needs and wants? How important and valuable do you think you are in the greater scheme of things?

Life actually works the other way around. We exist in a benevolent Universe, which always gives us the consequences of our choices blended with what we need to evolve into our best self. If you can't perceive the gifts the Universe is trying to offer you, through the mirror of your life, then the problem is with you, not the Universe. Perhaps what you expect from life is contrary to the purpose of your existence. Like any wise parent, the Universe always loves us but will never support its Soul children making choices which do not support their evolution and the Divine Plan. If you feel you have nothing to be grateful for, then your alignment is completely out of whack. Perhaps you need to update what you consider to be the gifts of life…

Gratitude helps you realign to Universal Truth and Divine benevolence. You don't need an external reason to be grateful. Like every attitude or response to life, we can simply choose gratitude. If you look through the eyes of the Soul, there is always something you can be grateful for. A simple gratitude journey is a common exercise to start this off. Make the effort to remember the blessings in your life, starting with those easily taken for granted by the entitled soul: food on your plate, a roof over your head, the presence of friends or family, your pet, the sun shining outside, beautiful flowers in the local park, a nice neighbour, having a job that allows you to pay your bills….etc. Noticing all the small blessing we forgot to pay attention to is an easy way to begin reorienting our consciousness towards perceiving the many gifts that surround us.

The next step would then be to be grateful for things that can seem more difficult to be grateful for. The bills that you have to pay are something you can be grateful for, because paying an electricity bill means you have electricity, provided for you through the work of others. Paying taxes means you are earning money and are in a position to contribute to society (this is aside from any political discussion about how governments may use or misuse public funds). Can you see how it is all in your perspective? Things don't have to be perfect or ideal to carry a gift. Once we bring gratitude into the mix, the energy of our relationship with the object of gratitude rises in vibration, flows better and becomes more productive of love rather than unnecessary hardship. Gratitude is an easy way to bring love to the un-loveable.

Learning to be grateful for the difficult things in life, including pain, failure and loss, is where your gratitude muscle will be most tested. Yet, this is where gratitude is at its most transformational. Adopting gratitude towards the painful and challenging experiences of life requires the will to choose receptiveness to the hidden gifts of the experience, thereby realigning us towards evolutionary learning. It is okay to feel all the other angry, hurt feelings too, but we can't stay bogged in bitterness and despair, for our own sake and the sake of those we love. We must becoming proficient at moving through the pained feelings and realign to being grateful for the experience of life and its lessons: What it is teaching us (even if we can't see it right off the bat)? What it is giving us the opportunity to face? How it is making us stronger? More compassionate? Wiser? What we turn the experience into is up to us. Will we turn it into love? or into fear? There will always be a way to reorient our experience towards the creation of love. This is how we transform curses into blessings. Gratitude helps us to grow up spiritually. It frees us to move forward into a new phase of a journey where all our experiences contributed something of value.

The Universe is not incompetent. Regardless of the packaging, nothing happens without a benevolent evolutionary reason, though the reason may not be obvious to us at first. Eventually, if we remember that the goal of existence is not to "feel good and live happily forever after" but to evolve, and if we allow ourselves to realign to this fundamental truth for our very existence, then gratitude will be our best friend in taking life in and transforming it into love. Gratitude can be quite magical. By putting your will behind the choice to be grateful, thus aligning yourself to the benevolence of the Universe, you will begin to see things as God sees it. You will be able to partner better with God-Goddess and your Soul Tree, as they seek to teach and nurture you, little leaf.

- Love Yourself yet Be Selfless

This statement sums up the healthy balance of self-esteem in spiritual initiates. Becoming less self-absorbed, more altruistic, but without being a doormat, is paramount in the realignment towards unity-consciousness and spiritualised ideals. Selfish egos think mostly about themselves. Spiritualised humans think in terms of the highest good of all concerned, but some forget that "all concerned" includes ourselves! Just as those who are selfish and self-oriented are far from any spiritualised state, those who constantly deny, mistreat and martyr themselves in the name of service are also not in the correct alignment to Service. The key is to hold a fine balance between loving yourself, yet being selfless.

We must know and prove ourselves to be worthy in order to feel comfortable taking our place and playing our part in the Divine Plan. In order to be sucked into place by the Universe, we must also relinquish selfishness and self-interest in dedication to serving to highest good of All. This requires a finely balanced cocktail of self-love, self-respect, self-care and unconditional positive regard towards the self. It also requires the love of our fellow men and creatures, and the desire to nurture their evolution and spiritual well-being.

Please be aware that indulging our ego is not self-love. Pleasing our ego may feel good in the short term, but harms our eternal well-being. And while self-care routines like a bit of rest and a nice hot bath can contribute to self-care, self-love goes much further. Love is that which nurtures evolution. Self-love is treating ourselves in ways which nurture our evolution. Being selfless means that we commit and dedicate ourselves to being of greatest service, even if it means making personal sacrifices in order to fulfil our duty of spiritual care. These are simple concepts to grasp in theory, but, in practice, it is not always simple to master the balance between these two states. It takes time, application, honest self-reflection, and review. It is something that a teacher or mentor can support you with as they mirror for you any imbalances in this dynamic.

- Be Solution-Oriented
This is a simple yet profound reorientation. People who see only problems will get more problems and get

nowhere. Problem-finders can't see past the mountains that life challenges us to climb, and so they stop moving forward and give up.

Every question has an answer and every problem a solution. The answer may not be easy, the solution may not be ideal, but it will be there. Be willing to look past the obvious, think outside of the box and be creative if need be. Don't be defeatist, have a can-do attitude and simply make it so. The achievement of Spiritual Mastery and Ascension is never easy. We must decide in advance that we will get through, learn from and tackle every challenge that presents, because we know that the Universe never presents us with anything we can't handle. This is Universal Law. Being defeatist means you focus on all the reasons why you can't do something; All you need is one good valid reason why you can! Find a way, and if you can't find a way, create one.

The other side of this coin is that the means don't always justify the end. You must at all times overcome challenges not by any means necessary, but with wisdom, illumined intelligence and guided by the spiritual intelligence of the Soul Tree. Those who follow the philosophy of "the end justifies the means" can become so tunnel-vision focused on their goal that they become blind to the harm they cause to get there. This is not the work of a spiritual initiate. While some goals may demand some sacrifices, we must always remain in compassion and guided by higher love, not driven by the hunger for success. Selfish ambition is a sin, not a masterful quality. You must always uphold a good standard of ethical behaviour and find the solution which will serve the highest good of All concerned..

- Study

If you want to be successful at anything, you must study the theory as well as put it into practice. Many of the strategies describes so far - energy hygiene, attitude of gratitude, meditation, review or self-reflection - are practical elements of the curriculum. We can address the theoretical aspect of our learning through spiritual reading, research or doing workshops, courses or training with spiritual facilitators and teachers. For a disciple consciously on the spiritual path, practice will be the most important aspect of growth, but there must be a certain amount of time dedicated to the study of spiritual or personal growth topics every week. As with anything in life, always be discerning and in your deeper heart's knowing as the honesty, clarity, ethics and wisdom of whatever you read or participate in. Everyone has something to offer, but that doesn't mean that everything they offer is clear or right (and yes, this applies to me too).

-Ask the Soul Tree to Guide You to Your Teacher

It is easy to add this request into your daily prayer practice, as it fits into the category of asking the Soul Tree to support your growth and evolution.

No one has ever achieved high levels of spiritual attainment by themselves. Everyone comes to a point in their life when they need to find a teacher or mentor. Such a teacher must be one who is a few steps ahead of us in the process of initiation, and who can pass on their wisdom from personal experience. This is how the circle of life works to serve our evolution: we are all connected, and we are all part of a greater Unity where every part serves the other parts. Those a few steps ahead help those who are a few steps behind, and so on. Every teacher has their own teacher, and every student will, in time, have their own students - whether this is in a formal teaching setting or manifests in other ways.

While we are individual aspects of Source, we are also part of something larger. No one is an island and the more advanced we become on the initiation path, the more group work and group processing becomes a central part of the journey.

When the student is ready, the teacher presents. A little help can't hurt though.. Ask daily for your Soul Tree, your Higher Self, to help guide you to your teacher, and to help you recognise them when you find them. This is good practice for those searching for their teacher. You must remain in tune enough to follow the guidance each step of the way. The teacher may come to you, or you may have to go to your teacher. Be patient and follow the higher guidance of your Soul Tree, and your spiritual intuition. Don't discount seemingly small internal nudges to go places or to do certain things that may seem innocuous. Profound encounters can happen in the most unexpected places.

I would strongly advice to make sure that the teachers you meet have a good track record of ethical conduct, abstaining from spiritually harmful behaviours such as casual sex with students, drugs, alcohol, financial abuse or power manipulation. Remember that there are plenty of false prophets out there. Make sure you don't rush into anything out of desperation or urgency, but don't hold back when you find the teacher who is right for you.

RESOURCE:
DAILY MEDITATION

PROTECTION, VIOLET FLAME AND ALIGNEMENT TO THE SOUL TREE

Find a private and contained space where you will not be disturbed. You can stand, sit, recline, be cross-legged or lay down for this, but don't fall asleep! Although you may enter an altered state which can almost feel dreamlike during meditation, there should still be a sense of awareness and engagement. You may hold a crystal or two in your hands if you feel to, as crystals can be a great help in intensifying and focusing energy, attuning to Gaia, and integrating energy at the physical level.

Begin with taking a series of slow, conscious breaths to slow down and anchor yourself here now, fully present in your body, in this space, in this moment. Release all tension and distractions. Settle in your body and close your eyes.

Feel into your heart centre, the energy vortex at the centre of your chest. Feel the love present in this space. If your heart is open today, the love will easily be felt. If your heart is less open today, you may have to reach a little deeper into this centre to access the presence of love which exists there. Simply know that it is always there. Take a few moments to just be in your heart space, to anchor your heart as your energetic centre, the centre of your energy focus in this body. I AM CENTRED WITHIN MY HEART.

After a little while, visualise a bright, strong, impenetrable bubble of golden light, all around you, your aura and four-body system. Feel and assert that this bubble of golden light is a shield of absolute protection around your energy, protecting you from all that is less than unconditional love. It protects your physical, emotional, lower mental and Buddhic vehicles. From your centre, affirm that you choose to love and care for yourself. Within your energy, set and intend the holding strong personal and spiritual boundaries based on unconditional love, which allow only unconditional love to be shared and exchanged. Feel this. MY PROTECTION AND BOUNDARIES ARE ABSOLUTE IN LOVE AND LIGHT.

I REFUSE ALL COMMUNICATIONS WHICH ORIGINATE UPON THE ASTRAL PLANE.

Now, visualise a strong column of white light extending from your heart centre, down your body, down your legs and going down your grounding cord into the Earth, all the way to the core of the Earth like a big root of light. Feel your energy being magnetically pulled and grounded properly into your body, and anchored in the Earth. Be here now. I AM GROUNDED INTO THE EARTH. I AM HERE NOW.

Now, visualise the column of white light also extending from your heart centre upwards, through your head, extending out from your Crown chakra at the top of your head, and up into your connection with your Soul Tree. Reach up as high as you can reach with the intention to connect with and align to your Soul Tree's energy and guidance. I AM ALIGNED TO MY HIGHER SELF. I AM RECEPTIVE TO HIGHER LOVE AND HIGHER TRUTH.

Now, as you central column of light is strong and aligned, and you are centred in your heart, call forth the Violet Flame with your mind, feelings and intention.

Visualise this violet fire energy. Connect to it and ask for a shower and deep penetration of the Violet Flame throughout your entire energy field and four-body system. Visualise a wide stream and shower of violet fire energy pouring and flowing deeply into and through your energy system. See, know and feel it penetrating everywhere physically, emotionally, mentally and at individual soul level, and then flowing through you into the Earth, with gratitude. Feel the Violet Flame burning up the dross, transmuting all negativity and fear, dissolving limitations and barriers, raising your vibration and purifying your energy at every level. Direct a focus of it towards any area of disharmony within you if necessary. Be in acceptance, breathe and release. Stay with this focus for a little while, as guided, allowing the Violet Flame to clear your energy field. Remember to allow, accept and let go as much as you can with anything which is no longer serving your evolution, and anything which is an energy lesser than unconditional love. I RELEASE ALL THAT NO LONGER SERVES ME, WITH LOVE

While you can allow the Violet Flame to keep running through your energy, put your focus back now on your central column of white light, with your and your heart at the centre of the bridge of light running from your Higher Self, down through your being and heart centre, and into the Earth. Visualise and feel this columns becoming stronger, clearer and wider until it encircles your entire energy system. Open yourself to your Higher Self, its influence and guidance. Have no expectation. Simply be open and receptive to its energy and anything else which may need and be ready to be shared or downloaded. Enjoy communing and being with the energy of your Soul Tree for a while.

I CALL FORTH THE PROTECTION AND GUIDANCE OF THE GREAT SPIRITS OF LOVE,

LIGHT AND TRUTH FROM THE HIGHER
MENTAL PLANE AND BEYOND. I HUMBLY
AND GRATEFULLY RECEIVE.

MAY LOVE RESTORE THE BALANCE!

When the time feels right, gently wrap up your
meditation by expressing gratitude to all the energies
which assisted you in this meditation. Open your eyes,
and allow yourself to feel different and be different as
you go forth into your day. Make you sure bubble of
protection is still in place, and that you are properly
grounded, stable and centred in your body before
walking off to face your day. THANK YOU.

CHAPTER 7

Conclusion: It's Only The Beginning…

~~~

Once upon a time, I received a calling from my Soul Tree. I was wise enough to answer it, and chose to walk the road less travelled. What a journey it has been! And it's not over yet, as I slowly explore my way up the Tree of Life in this wondrous, multi-dimensional Creation. I have come a long way, and yet I have so much more to learn. I almost always feel like a beginner in my life, but it is only because I am growing into new horizons. That's the point!

Is there something more to life than the tick-tock of normal material living? Is there more to life than getting a job, having a family and looking forward to your next holiday? The answer is a resounding YES…. But only if you have the wherewithal to listen to the whispers of your Soul Tree.

The concrete and material plane of existence is in fact a tiny part of what Life is all about. The experience of the body-mind spans across only three levels of the 352 levels of experience that this Creation has to offer. It's a small world indeed for those whose consciousness is entombed in the world of matter! Those who let themselves be lulled into spiritual sleep forget their spiritual origins and lose themselves in the heresy of the physical senses. Such souls end up living lives that sustain them as creatures, but starve them as Souls. Third-dimensional entrapment is encouraged by a world system which wants us to be disconnected from our Source. It makes us better consumers, and easier to control, but it makes commitment to the spiritual path more difficult as so many are distracted by the glitz and glamour of our modern civilisation.

I refused the collective push towards existing as a body-mind living unconsciously. I answered the call to wake up. If you have read up to this point, there is a good chance you feel the same way. The truth is, regardless of the challenges on the way, we never feel better or more in place than when we answer the higher calling to evolve and fulfil our spiritual destiny. It is not an easy path, but it is the answer to the empty hole that most spiritually unconscious people feel inside themselves.

The insights shared in this book offer a foundational understanding of our place within the larger design of a living, evolving Creation. The symbology of the Tree of Life is commonly used to represent the wonderful, interconnected complexity of the larger Being that we are a part of. I hope that, through your reading, you felt the recognition in your heart and Soul of a Truth calling out to you, through your own Higher Self. As we know, reading a book is not enough to integrate and master a subject. Theory is one thing, but practice is where the theory falls into place and becomes useful. Everyone can cram their monkey mind full of interesting information, but unless it helps you change and grow in a real embodied way, it's just more noise in your mental library. No transformation can happen simply by understanding something with your mind. Transformation must be lived, felt and experienced on every levels of our being in a way which alters us in tangible ways.

I have shared some useful tips and exercises to get you started, but one can only go so far without a teacher and a group of other like-minded initiates. You may feel guided to look around for a guide or teacher you have not met yet. But if the information and energy shared in this book resonated with you, then perhaps you want to take your next steps onto the path of Personal Spiritual Alchemy with us, our team at the Cosmosis® Mentoring Centre,

We have many services on offer, some of them free and available to anyone in the world, from any location as long as you have internet access. We are a group of like-minded souls who have walked the path of spiritual growth, service and spiritual alchemy for many years in this life, and many lifetimes before this ones. We are devoted to helping others actualise their Divine potential for Mastery through the Transformation through Mastery approach. We combine ancient wisdom and mystical teachings with the modern professionalism of mentoring, coaching and counselling skills. We are a community of qualified individuals in the helping professions, because anyone serious about God realisation will at different times in the journey require the support of varied approaches and modalities. As far as our work goes, it includes mentoring, coaching, training, teaching, healing, natural health support, counselling and psychological therapy.

If you are interested to find out more, please explore the contents of our website, and try our free introductory services. There is no coercion, no manipulation, no weirdness. We simply offer a path, and it's up to you to decide if it feels right to study with us for a short time, a long time or not at all. We have one of the strictest and most professional codes of ethics and professional conduct among spiritual groups and do not tolerate behaviours such as casual sex, drug use, unhealthy power dynamics or financial corruption. We do our very best to walk the talk of our spiritual ideals and ethical values, in every area of our life.

For success on this path, we must be a good match for you, and you must be a good match for the work we do. The best way to find out if we're a good fit is to try it out and see how you go. If it doesn't work for you, then you can go on your merry way and find your bliss elsewhere. If you resonate with our introductory teachings and find that they benefit you, then you may want to sign up for our global mentoring programme of study.

Our Website
For more information on us and our services, go to our website for the Cosmosis® Mentoring Centre: **www.mysteryschool.au**

Free weekly online class and free online courses
A great way get a beginner taste for what we offer is to participate in our free weekly online class, or try our free online courses. You will find the information about these free services under our 'Services' page on our website.

Our weekly global online classes are facilitated by members of our team of professionally qualified mentors and senior students. They involve the playing of a recording from classes taught by our main teachers, followed by a group discussion and exploration.

Our free online courses cover several foundational areas of our beginner teachings: energetic hygiene, abundance and gratitude, working with the violet flame, worthiness, pitfalls on the path, and self-esteem. You go through these online courses at your own pace, and are assigned one of our mentors as a point of contact. You may email them if you have any questions or need anything, and they may occasionally check on you to see how you are going.

Online Shoppe

Our online shop offers a range of resources for you to purchase, including books from our Insight Series, as well as CDs and DVDs containing the recordings of classes and teaching sessions. Go to: https://mysteryschool.au/shoppe/

YouTube

Our YouTube channel features a large amount of video processes which can be another great way to explore some of our work for free. Please be aware that the energetic processing and support we offer our students is more intensive than what you will experience through our open-source services.

Visit:

https://www.youtube.com/@Cosmosismentoring

"The Basic Science of Ascension" by Michael King, which I mentioned in chapter 2, is currently to be found here:

https://www.youtube.com/watch?v=lf2bvBnozHk . If this link changes over time, simply search for it by name on our YouTube channel.

Facebook

Of course, we can also be found on Facebook: **www.facebook.com/Cosmosismentoring/**
****

As you can see, there is plenty to sink your teeth into in order to get an introductory experience of the Path of Personal Spiritual Alchemy with us. If you find all these resources valuable, then perhaps you will be ready to embark on this wonderful journey with the Cosmosis® team supporting you along the way. Our mentoring programme offers gradual progression through increasingly more advanced levels of mentoring. We have a team of professionally qualified mentors, all long-time students bound by our code of ethics, who will walk by your side at every step, as you progress on this path. I and the other core teachers facilitate regular classes, workshops and intensives for our students. We're all just doing our best to serve our evolution, serve the evolution of others, and support this beautiful little planet and Her evolution.

… Are you ready to find that something more?

ABOUT THE AUTHOR

~~~

Segolene King is a spiritual teacher, and a professionally qualified personal growth mentor, life coach and trainer.

Born and bred in France, Segolene spent her late teens and young adult years juggling university studies and travel in search of both herself and her life path. She embarked consciously on the Path of Personal Spiritual Alchemy is 2004, after meeting her husband and old Soul friend Michael King.

She now lives in Australia with her family. In her work, she supports students around the world, and serves as the Chief Mentor and Operations Manager with the Cosmosis® Mentoring Centre.

www.segolene.com.au

www.mysteryschool.au